Horsemanship
The Revelations

Holly Davis

Copyright © 2014 Holly Davis

All Rights Reserved.

ISBN-10: 1507753950
ISBN-13: 978-1507753958

This book may not be reproduced in whole or part in any form or by any means, electronic, mechanical, or otherwise without permission from the Author. Except by a reviewer, who may quote brief paragraphs in a review.

For all other permissions, please contact the Author

www.hollydavis.co.uk

DEDICATION

For all of the people that are seeking a better way
forwards – those with open hearts and minds.

For my own horses - both past and present.

For the horses heard and the horses that scream –
may you be heard – may change come.

With much love and gratitude for all horses.
Whoever and wherever they may be.

ACKNOWLEGEMENTS

Cover Photograph
Tim Duckworth at Bitless and Barefoot
From the Arabian Nights Collection

Photographs
Bitless and Barefoot
Camille Dareau

Foreword
Avis Senior
BHSAI
Author of Horse Riding – Choose Your Weapons

Contributor
Camille Dareau
Happy Horse Training

CONTENT

Foreword..1

Introduction...3
The Equestrian Deception......................10
The Ghost in the Machine.....................22
Sympathy VS Empathy.........................29
Looking Glass Syndrome......................33
Equine Autism and Learning Difficulties.......38
Equine Mental Illness..........................48
Neonatal Maladjustment Syndrome............55
The Horse in Pain...............................78
No Bit, no Brakes................................95
Is your Horses Bit Affecting Their Hearing?...107
Bitless Bridles..................................110
The False Guru.................................119
The True Horseman............................129
Static Objects on Moving Backs..................136
Static Riders....................................143
Rugging and Clipping..........................155
The Importance of Vitamin D..................171
Mudfever and Scratches........................175
The Olfactory System..........................180
Seaweed..186
Stabling vs Freedom of Movement..............193
The Horse's Energy Awareness..................202

About the Author...............................208
Resources.......................................211

FOREWORD

I was particularly honoured and humbled when Holly Davis asked if I would write a foreword for her latest work 'Horsemanship – The Revelations'. We met through Social Media some months before when our respective careers and energies became entwined.

We had done a 'book swap' – Holly's 'Energy Healing for Horses – A Comprehensive Guide to Learning' in return for my equestrian guide 'Horse Riding Choose Your Weapons'.

I too am an Animal Communicator and Energy Healer; however, within a few lines of reading, my mind was embroiled in a whole new world I never knew existed; a world far in advance of my own knowledge of intuitive communication and healing.

So of course, I knew the title 'Horsemanship – the Revelations' would fill me with as much awe and I looked forward to receiving the draft.

Compelling, truthful and often heart wrenching are the words of 'Horsemanship – The Revelations'. Holly lays bare the innate abuse horses suffer at our physical, mental and emotional demands – deliberate or not - and the all-round care and handling regimes; the effects of which burn through the physical horse, tearing right through 'the inner horse - the invisible ghost'.

There is far more to the horse than most of us realise or accept. I defy anyone to read 'Horsemanship – the Revelations' and not be humbled enough to seek 'the invisible ghost'.

**Avis Senior BHSAI,
Author of 'Horse Riding Choose Your Weapons**

INTRODUCTION

When I wrote the first book in the Horsemanship series, I was not aware of how popular this book would become in such a short time. It would appear that the doors in equestrianism are opening; along with the hearts and minds of those individuals ready and willing to seek the innate truth that is the horse.

Whilst when I started to write I was only too aware of how I may be questioned due to my lack of riding and competition interest, this has actually not been the case. Rather, my book has met with open minds and those willing and able to seek and explore further, as if pulled by an invisible force that all unites us in seeking the truth and the considering of what is truth for us today, may not be tomorrow. We are growing and learning at a rapid speed; one in which the horses gently and firmly pushes us forwards and nearer to both our own and their truth. It would appear that it is not now so much about how many hours we sit in the seat of our 'machine' that we clock up that counts, but instead, the insights that we gain quite simply just whilst in quiet presence of the horse.

How many of us stop to consider something so simple as how we breathe in the presence of our horses? How the simplicity of 'breath' can lower heart rate, blood pressure, reduce stress and bring calm? Breathing is the very essence of our being; the oxygen that feeds body and brain and help fulfil the senses. When we breathe in unison our body's synchronise, work together and the rider and horse become the Centaur. No separation; no aids other than those subconscious cues that we offer each other. Rather than just fumbling bodies trying to move together and guess the next move of the other in a bid to keep balance in order to reach a perceived finish line that brings ribbons.

Many of the readers of this book will have heard the term 'be' with your horse. How many of us understand what it is to 'be'? Why 'being' is so important? And yet it is the foundation of everything we could/should do within the company of our horses. The 'being' that enables firm foundations to be laid for the future that is to come to remain solid, secure, and viable without the need for pain and control.

With so many equestrians, awakening questions are now being asked. Questions such as is it ethical to tie down horses? Some are even questioning if we have the right to ride horses at all!
Where ever you are and whatever your questions, the fact you are questioning and holding this book in your hands is a sign of awakening; a sign that you are now moving closer to understanding the language that is Equus and the messages and teachings that this brings.

None of us were born 'knowing' what to do and how to think with regards to horses. But with a compassionate and open mind, slowly and surely we are all learning, and the doors are opening to new insights that only the horse can bring. We only have to look to Equine Facilitated Therapy to see the huge and often so profound impact the horse can have on our emotional state through his guidance. How horses are helping us to heal as they whisper quietly the words needing to be heard by those ready and willing to listen. These sessions are co-ordinated; set up for this purpose and yet....just taking a stroll to the field to 'be' with your horse, observe, engage in the shared offerings and interactions and peace, is in itself healing and can bring so much if not more so.

We have chosen our horses for a reason; we have been drawn to those individuals that suit us through resonance attraction. There is an unspoken acknowledgment that they need us also - a true partnership in the making. But in order to reach this goal - this oneness - many questions need to be asked, knowledge gained and whispers heard and acknowledged. In order to get here we must cast aside our own agendas, consider our dreams, needs, and desires and analyse them and what is behind them in great detail. Failure to do so and not being truthful to ourselves is just as much a curse to our horse as it is to ourselves. How can he know you if you do not know yourself? How can he trust you if you cannot trust yourself? How can you sleep at night through your worry? How can he, as he will feel it too.

In truth he asks very little from you; certainly nothing that is unobtainable for you to achieve. Quite simply he seeks the heart of a lion with the gentleness of the lamb. The open minded truth seeker that quietly listens, observes and considers his side as well as your own. Is that really too much for him to ask of you? Can you keep him safe in times of stress and fulfil his physical and emotional needs when he too chooses to heal and become the horse he was always destined to be? A journey shared together with a common goal; one of freedom from restraint and conditioning. A freedom that allow expression, play and evolvement each and every day. Progression not just in our equestrian skills, but also in self mastery to enable him to look to us as we do to him. A life and relationship based on mutual truth and trust. Of course our backgrounds are different; our own being predatory and his of the prey. But this is of little concern once the deal has been sealed and we have found our balance in trust.

The tide is turning; hearts are opening and truly acknowledging the relationships, trust and insights that are being offered by our equine friends for our own growth. Slowly disappearing are the days where abuse of these majestic creatures is accepted; the voices and minds are learning and open to speaking out for them. Backs are turning, and condemned to the bin are the leather straps that have kept their voices from being heard for far too long. The horse's voice is multiplying; people are questioning as if 100th monkey syndrome is playing out in the equestrian world. Whispers carry on the wind, heard by those open and willing to entertain the ideas and feelings of the sentient horses that have come to teach, inspire and befriend us.

Listen to the whispers, as only too often those whispers are that which are so important; the subtleties offered for those who quietly listen. Let us no longer create a world where the horse needs to scream. Let us go to him quietly, heart and mind open and offering to hear what needs to be voiced; that we may make the changes our heart knows are needed and let our mind show us the way through that heart felt connection. There is no excuse, no excuse at all not to 'hear', we all have that ability and that ability is a gift, a gift that can and does create change each and every day. Let us, through the horse, learn about our authentic self, let him be our guide on this journey, enabling him to point out when we stray from the path, with no fear of punishment when he 'shouts' to call us back onto that path from which we have strayed.

In this alien world of the predator in which he lives and breathes, let him find his peace and his place at your side. He is learning just as you are. You have invited him into your world and asked him for those times spent together, to step out of his own. What a privilege for us when he chooses to stand at our side so willingly!

He is our teacher; our faithful friend and at times our protector. Let us too extend him the hand of friendship and honor his gifts offered to us by exchange of our own in return. That of peace, comfort and equality - we do not and we cannot 'own' him. Ownership is just a state of mind and means nothing over and beyond law and intent. Rather, he is quite simply his own person, one that should not be denied and ignored as a sentient living breathing being that he is. When we enable and 'allow' this concept to come to mind we view him in a whole new light; one of the giving, wholesome creature that he so authentically is and offers himself to you as. He offers you all that he is in each given moment; he does not lie, steal or try to cheat you. He does not get it wrong - it is just that sometimes he is unable to offer that which you desire or that you have instructed him incorrectly. His reluctance and lack of response is only his cue for you to search outside of the box and find the answer to your posed question to him.

He seeks your acknowledgment always, your voice to him that 'yes' this is what I am asking 'thank you' and what can I offer you by way of balance. You can and are changing his life with each interaction experienced between you, however great or small. Each day brings lessons anew, knowledge to be sought and realisations to be gleamed, each a gift in themselves, even the hard ones.

He does not have to comply when pressure is applied to him physically or emotionally; he makes his choice to be with you - what an honor!

Let us as a whole hear them; learn from them and engulf them in respect!

THE EQUESTRIAN DECEPTION

The sad truth is that the world of equestrianism has been deceiving us for many decades; centuries in fact. Even in our modern world of advanced understanding of behaviour and psychology, it is still taught that it is perfectly acceptable to abuse a horse. This may be in the form of whips, spurs, hands, metal bits and all manner of tack set up to 'control' and restrict the freedom and expression that is the horse. The law allows it to continue with no laws being created and implemented in such a way as to protect these humble beings from the harsh reality of primeval humans that insist that 'the horse must be controlled'. If only these same people would stop and look into their hearts and learn to feel with them; then they would be able to see the reality of what just hands and voice alone can do. The hands that hit and hold the whip; the voice that causes the horses guts to lurch and tremble inside at the mere notion that this being is close by and likely about to strike and cause both mental and physical pain. These same people that are creating depression, anxiety and mental illness in our horses; they are taking part and engaging in abuse.

Think for a moment if you will lifting a whip to a puppy or digging him in the side with a spur....acceptable? No of course not, but for many this is the everyday accepted behaviour and abuse inflicted on our horses. Inflicted by adults that should know better and by children that have not been raised to respect the magnificent inner being of the horse. Not to mention the so called 'professional' that has to jab and beat the horse as a way of making him bend to his will in the name of coloured ribbons. The same ribbons kids win every weekend through abusing their ponies pushed on by over baring parents that are unable to have their children be seen to fail in public.

Parents that spend thousands on ponies that have earned their name in the show ring and now must prove the same all over with their own child. In fact, maybe we should even stop and consider that the teaching of abuse and pressure on a young child in itself is child abuse? The same children we are meant to bring up with good morals and ethics to help them through life and not harm. These same children are being taught how to inflict pain with no remorse and no feeling. What kind of message are we then sending out?

These children are the new generation and the ones that can create change. Little hope is there for the horse when the new generation is not only being deceived, but openly being encouraged to behave in such a manner. Continuing to be taught that abuse is an acceptable part of riding and ownership. Shame on those adults that should and do know better but continue regardless, allowing the corruption of young minds and continual assault against the horse. The tide is turning; both new and old generations alike are beginning to awaken. No longer is the showing world only full of the 'controllers'. Quietly, but surely, the new breed of equestrian is breaking into the showing and competition world. Quietly going about their business and leading by example. Rather than telling others they are 'wrong', instead, showing how it can be done 'correctly' with love and respect of horses. These people are raising eyebrows; they are causing questions to be asked. These are the people creating change in their own way; the ones that are not at war with the horse, rather, searching for the quiet content of partnership within the show ring and it is starting to be seen and questioned.

When we choose to stand back and acknowledge that it is the taking part that counts, that we can not 'win' off another's back, the agenda cracks and falls away. The enjoyment comes as does the partnership, and the natural flow and enjoyment materialise in place of the stress, yanking and determination to win at any cost to the horse that stands beneath us.

How many of us stop to consider something so simple as how we breathe in the presence of our horses? How the simplicity of 'breath' can lower heart rate, blood pressure, reduce stress and bring calm? Breathing is the very essence of our being; the oxygen that feeds body and brain and helps fulfil the senses. When we breathe in unison our body's synchronise, work together, and the rider and horse become the Centaur. No separation; no aids other than those subconscious cues that we offer each other. Rather than just fumbling bodies trying to move together and guess the next move of the other in a bid to keep balance in order to reach a perceived finish line that brings ribbons.

It takes little emotional intelligence and common sense to both consider and know that the horse 'feels'. He is made of blood, flesh, bone and nerve endings just the same as we are. He possesses all of the same emotional chemicals that we do; both in his brain, and in every organ of his body. He feels pain, he grieves, he can become depressed and he knows fear to no lesser degree than we do. Further to this in an alien world controlled by humans, his predators, the anxieties and fears can grow. He is our horse; he does as he is told and only too often does he not even know he is allowed to question and have a voice.

Thanks to the technology of the modern world and social media, much of this abuse is now being exposed. The Rollkur of the dressage world and the photographs of so called 'professionals' that abuse are being exposed publicly and yet...still it continues due to a minority of hearts and minds that still remain closed. These are the so called professionals that so many look to and are inspired by. The same people that are teaching that abusing a horse at whatever cost to their welfare is acceptable. Yet times are on the change; it never has been nor will it ever be acceptable and one day these people will know that. The doors will close on them and the crowds will turn their backs to them; it is already beginning to happen. It will continue to happen as the equestrian world wakes to the being that is the humble horse, and learns to respect that which is innate to them, the feeling of peace without conflict.

Let us take a look at Dressage; so often we see horses with mouths clamped shut and struggling to breathe. Necks cranked in in an unnatural and painful position we are told is 'correct'. No consideration for the individual's conformation, muscle tone and strength being taken into account. We are simply taught and believe that this unnatural outline behind the vertical is 'correct' and that if we wish to 'win' it is what we must aspire to achieve, regardless of our horse's welfare.

No doubt there will be those that feel I am singling out Dressage; that is not my intention at all. It is purely that this is a discipline that so widely accepts cruelty as the norm. Take away the mouth clampers, the double bridles and how many of these professionals can truly ride? How many of their horse's would still hold respect for them in newly found freedom? How many of these horses will know how to maintain their frame correctly when no longer artificially held in place? How many of those Dressage professionals can rise to the trot in the absence of their saddle?

One day the bleeding scar tissued mouths that are common today will be cast to the past where they belong and there they will stay. No longer will it be accepted as part of riding; no longer will it be seen as the norm. Rather, it will be condemned as what in truth it is - abuse, unacceptable and the result as a corruptive bygone era that has no place in equestrianism and partnership today.

All too often though, it is not just the Dressage rider that harms with their hands. Rough hands and bleeding mouths are common place throughout the ridden horse world. Not all created through determination to win at all cost, but also through fear, ignorance and lack of knowledge. Whilst these are reasons, these reasons no longer hold water when the truth and information is out there, we only need to look and ask for help, it is out there, and we can create change.

One day it will no longer be accepted the norm for the show jumper to have his head held in as he jumps and tries to clear and land safely. He will not have to create artificial balance each time he leaps due to the shortness of the reins. Instead, he will be offered freedom in natural balance as his rider learns to trust and let go of control in order that he may carry them both safely to the other side.

An instructor once told me a story: A man turned up to begin learning to ride, along with his horse and tack. The instructor asked him 'do you need that saddle and bridle?' The man replied that he did. The instructor then told him he could not have it, that it would be returned to him when it was not needed. In three lessons that man learnt to ride with more natural balance than many professionals will ever obtain. I cannot say that I am surprised in this at all. As all too often the saddle, stirrups and the reins are used to maintain artificial balance and once removed the lack of balance is all too easily seen.

The tack used, and ridden 'skills' to 'produce' the horse are so often sadly lacking from the innate formation and movement of the horse. When we remove the leather and metal, observe the horse with the respect for the innately beautiful being that he is, he will show us how he moves and how we can move with him without the need to control, restrict and force him. This is where the beauty then lies and will be seen and the dance between rider and horse begins, with clarity, respect and an open mind and heart. This goal can be reached; it is there waiting to be achieved by those that are free thinkers and feelers; those not afraid to go against the norm and give up their need to obtain ribbons; those that lead by example and remain true to our magnificent friends - the horses.

Imagine if those same ribbons were only handed to those deserving - how many eyebrows would be raised? I, like so many others, look forward to the day when judgment is removed from judging. When instead truth, natural balance and kindness is rewarded; when the saddle the horse wears, and the cost of the coat is no longer a consideration in how the awards are placed; the day judges stand up and demand that those that abuse leave the show ring and are asked not to return until they have learnt compassion. Will it ever happen? Maybe not within the next few years but it can when enough of us awaken, make a stand, and refuse to tolerate the abuse of the horse any longer.

Imagine a day the horse enters for his Dressage test with no bit in his mouth or leather strap around his nose. He creates his own outline slightly in front of the vertical and the dance begins. The request asked by his rider is willingly answered by the horse with no fear of punishment for refusal. The horse quite simply just offers his response to an only too natural request, why would he feel the need to refuse? Even wearing his bridle this same outcome may be achieved, quite simply, but the rider learning to be conscious of what their hands are doing and their hearts are feeling. The truth is the tack is of no harm to the horse when used correctly, so long as it is not deliberately created to harm just through the fitting - when the hands do not pull and the metal and leather do not dig. The harm rather comes from the hands that hold the reins, the unrelenting jabbing and pulling used to replace the true understanding of the art of ridden work and how it should and can be achieved with kindness and compassion.

Hands that pull and jab attach to the arms of the fearful rider. The one that fears failure, or the one that has set his agenda and intends to stick to it. Hands that hold tightly are not relaxed nor is the body that they are attached too. Chances are, nor is that rider breathing in a natural manner needed to correctly circulate oxygen around their body. Their core is likely held in by tension as the body forgets to breathe as the mind is not focused. The true concept of what the rider is looking to achieve has been forgotten is even given no mind at all.

Where has the freedom gone? The enjoyment? It has been replaced by stiff bodies that are fighting against each other in competition over making the other comply, more often than not the rider will be the one that wins this battle.

The rider breathes.... by way of response his horse breathes also. The hands that hold the reins lose their firm grip, and lightness has entered the mind and heart. The rider feels it and his horse responds as each begins to breathe in unison. The fear lessens; no longer is there need to fear, there never truly was - it was just perception. Together they are now learning what it is to win and truly master, enabling the ride to form the natural dance of the Centaur. Cast away is the fear, doubt and struggle of the fearful rider. Instead it is replaced with open mind and heart as taught by his trusted horse beneath him that has been screaming to be heard for so long.

This is the true 'win' and when achieved never will fail again. We simply just return to our horse as the willing student open and willing to hear the lesson for the day that is so openly being offered.

It is not only Dressage, the show ring and jumping arena where abuse is seen and accepted; it is in all areas and disciplines. When children are taught compassion and 'feel' it will enable them to grow into decent human beings that then are able to go on and enable their own children the same. What hope do children and horses have when raised by parents with small minded mentality? Those that push their children and their ponies before they are ready. Trussing them up in gag bits to slow them down and spurs to speed them up. Creating the constant push and pull on their ponies faces, causing pain and confusion.

At the time of writing this book my granddaughter is almost eight and she has never ridden a pony. Her experiences of horse back are on my 15.3hh Arabian. She has learnt to find her natural balance, release her fears and never has she gained the knowledge of artificial balance. Instead, she has learnt to move with my horse without the aid of tack - neither bridle nor saddle. This has helped her to kindly and naturally lay the foundations for the day her own young Arabian horse Harree is ready to begin his ridden education. Never will he know the harshness and cold of pulling metal over his bones, skin and nerves of his jaw, anymore than he will know tightness of reins and a jabbing of spurs. If only all children entered into the world of equestrianism like this so many equines would be spared abuse.

Once a child learns and understands the nature and natural flow that is the horse, why would they feel the need to abuse? Instead, let us help our children to understand that being an individual is alright. That there is nothing wrong with going against peer pressure but that there is harm in going against ones own truth. Horses have so much to offer our children - confidence, friendship and harmony and a desire for education knowledge, the simplistic but true kind. What a gift the horse has to offer them when enabled to do so!

Sadly, the truth in so many of the facilities and teachings for children and their ponies are not set up to facilitate this. Instead they are so often pushed into a competitive world right from the off. In my early equestrian years I once borrowed a friends pony and took both Gwinny and my daughter to the local Pony Club. What I witnessed there that day horrified me and we never returned. How dare that arrogant excuse for a horse woman think it Ok to walk into the arena and strike Gwinny with a whip! Sadly this is the controlling mentality of many of the Children's Pony Clubs set up by local hunts in existence today. That does not do much for the education of both equine and a child alike, does it?

THE GHOST IN THE MACHINE

How many of us stop to consider what consciousness is and how we think beyond the physical brain? The brain is simply a tool that retrieves, receives, and passes information. It is not the consciousness that makes us who we are; though how it is formed and wired will have an affect on how we think and perceive.

If we choose to view the conscious as the inner being - the thinking and feeling part of us - then we have to also accept that we are not the only species that experiences this. Whilst we may be standing at the side of our physical horse, there is also more that we are unable to see - that being the ghost in the machine that is the horse's consciousness.

The expression of self that comes from the consciousness can be both nurtured and destroyed, not just by the negative perception and thought of the individual, but also by the individual's experiences and interactions with others.

Why have I -chosen this title? Simple- the view of so many in the equestrian world is that the horse (to them) is little more than a machine - something to use and abuse and be forced to bend to their will. What they fail to see and acknowledge is the invisible ghost that dwells within. To acknowledge the existence of the horse's inner being, intellect, thoughts and feelings, means that so many would have to consider their own actions that are cruel, barbaric and against morality. For many it is so much easier to ignore this invisible ghost and to engage instead with the mechanical machine. This denial for many will mean that no guilt will, or can be felt by them through their actions towards the horse. How can there be if this denial exists? How can they harm a 'machine'?

It is the failing to acknowledge the ghost that is the inner horse that enables the abuse to continue. For many the machine is fed fuel and will not feel pain should the petrol run dry. At a later date it may be given an oiling and MOT when needed, thus saving it from the scrap yard that is the slaughterhouse. After all, you bought it, you need to make it last as long as you can to make sure you get your moneys worth!

A once a year MOT and service is not nearly enough. The horse needs correct fuel and nutrition all of the time. He needs his health issues to be treated and not just when they have gotten to a level that means he can not carry you on his back.

The other side of the coin is those that purposely go in search of the ghost in the machine. Those that know there is more to these unique beings and wish to understand them and what makes them tick. In truth, no two ghosts are the same. Yes, they may all have similar traits, but much of that will be down to conditioning and environment rather than nurture of the individual alone. For it is the nurturing of the individual, that enables the true personality to shine through. Not only this, but also the exploration of the inner self of the horse, by the horse.

This enables us to be attracted to the horses that we resonate with on a personal level, rather than those that just have the physical characteristics that we desire to fulfil our ego or agenda. This is how and when friendships and life long trust can be developed - healing starts.

If each time I had gone in search of a horse and just simply looked at the external machine, I would have walked away from each and every equine that has come into my care. I would have denied myself the insights and experiences that I have had; I would have spared myself tears and a small fortune financially. However, I would also not think and feel and be how I am today; I would have been emotionally denied by my own hand.

As the years have gone by I have no desire to ride, no desire to ask anything of my horses that they feel unable to do or are unable to offer. Why would I? Why would I force and manipulate my friends? This does not mean they are just field ornaments; instead we engage in mutual respect, groundwork and whatever they show me they need within their working life and when they are ready.

When my first mare arrived many years ago I was handed her bridle. I had never put a bridle on a horse before and pointed to the 'flash' and asked what it was for. It was explained to me, I removed it and I binned it. Her metal shoes and bit were to follow. The bit that she arrived with was too thick for her mouth and tongue. It was 'considered' kind as it was a snaffle. In fact it was a single jointed snaffle, the type that when the reins are used squeezes the tongue and hits the roof of the mouth – it was condemned to the bin. I still to this day struggle to understand why snaffles are considered kind when they are so deliberately designed to cause such discomfort, especially the single jointed variety. It took nothing more than someone to point out to me that horses were not born with metal on their feet. I removed her metal shoes and condemned those to the bin also. Before this time, being a novice caretaker, I just automatically thought that horses could not cope without shoes. Here begun my metal free life of horsemanship and my horse's freedom from iron.

It takes little consideration and common sense to make decisions such as these that are so firmly grounded in logic and compassion. Lets face it, horses managed rather well before humans came along and changed the goal posts that were to then force them into domestication and in some cases slavery. The least we can do is consider the horse in all of the decisions relating to his life experiences however numerous or minor they may be. That consideration, that acknowledgment is where truth will be learned and offered to us. Without that trust we run the risk of injury and chaos; maybe even a horse, damaged in both mind and spirit, homed by a rusty body, if he has not already closed down to the outside world and accepted his 'lot'.

When we choose to connect with the invisible ghost that is our horse, not only does this enable a new found unity to begin, but also insights will be gleamed and the lessons may begin. For some this may be the opening of the doors of spiritual awareness and healing that creates ripples through all aspects of their lives. Many will be drawn to learn and experience the art of just 'being' in the presence of their horse. It still amazes me that so many question what 'being' means and I can only assume that this means that they have yet to experience the inner ghost and being in his presence.

How can you teach this?

How can you teach someone to 'feel' and connect in this way?

This was a question I had some years ago to which I found a two fold answer. Firstly, you cannot 'teach' someone to 'feel'; it has to be an innate heart felt desire on their part. Secondly, once the student is ready, the horse will show them how. No effort is needed; just a little guidance as to how to go about it and then the horse's student from there, with guidance of their four legged friend, will find their way.

Many of my favourite and most insightful hours have been very late at night or very early morning, out in my fields under the moonlight. Many times all I chose to do was just sit on the fence and watch and observe my horses in those twilight hours. Sometimes they would just come and stand beside me and we would breathe together. This would cause ripples and goose bumps to travel right through my body. These kind offerings of their time and insights that my horses have shared with me have enabled me to relax, feel settled and to be myself. There is no judgment from horses towards us, they simply live in the moment and so often forgive the past. That does not mean that their anxieties of their last experiences have been forgotten and that their body's no longer react. But that it is 'forgiven' and no animosity is held towards the individual that may have wronged and harmed them.

If only more humans could feel and perceive as horses do!

Several years ago a lady booked to spend a day with me to learn animal communication. From the moment she stepped into my field it was apparent that my horses had other ideas, so we agreed to just go with the flow. At the end of the day I apologised to the lady as I had not taught her what she had come here to learn. She smiled and told me that she felt different from when she had arrived and that whatever it was that she had been seeking, she had found. Yet she said that if anyone were to ask her what that was, she would be unable to explain it beyond it being a *feeling*. I just smiled - I did not need to ask her what she meant. It would appear my horses had worked their magic yet again.

Experiencing the inner ghost of the horse is not something we can really describe in words beyond the word 'feeling'. It is either there or it isn't. It can not be faked and it cannot be forced. Actually once it is there, neither can it be denied, such is the power and yet quiet intensity of the feeling.

SYMPATHY VS EMPATHY

What we choose to work and how we think will have a huge impact on our emotional state when we are working with horses. Also, how we view them and how we cope with their illnesses and 'passings', as well as our emotional issues surrounding them.

Simply put, when we choose to work with sympathy, we leave ourselves open to be dragged into another's drama. We allow our own emotions to be affected by those of others. We finish our work, leave the company of that horse or person and we feel awful. We feel sad for their pain and we are worried about them. We can even have trouble sleeping through having them 'on our mind'. Whilst there is nothing wrong with sympathy in as much as it shows only too well the level of compassion innate to us, it does not serve us and nor is it positive for our own emotional health. It does not help the horses and people that may need our help and support and need us to be fully focused and present when we are in their company. If we are left worrying about a horse, that will be on our mind and our focus is not fully directed in the area that it needs to be when we are in the company of others. There are even instances when some horses and people may even feel patronised by another's sympathy towards them.

However, when we choose to work with empathy, this enables us to understand how the horse feels. At the same time it enables us to be able to safely guide our own emotions in such a way that we do not take the horse's negativity or sorrow upon ourselves. This enables us to support the individual with a positive outlook and approach, enabling us to help and inspire, as well as seeing the positive within a negative experience. It will stop us from being drained by their personal drama. By drama I am not insinuating in a patronising manner that they are creating drama. But rather, through circumstance, drama has manifested, not necessarily instigated by them and which may be beyond their control.

Empathy is supporting and creating an ideal that lacks and holds no agenda in changing another's life path, or interfering with it. It is the art of being able to play the observer, to watch, hear and understand what is playing out - without becoming directly involved. Working with empathy as the observer also enables us to stand back and see the bigger picture, rather than being directly emotionally involved. It aids us in being able to see things are they truly are and objectively. It enables us to view through the distortion of emotions, removing biased approach and outcome and gets us right to the heart of the matter.

When we let go of ego and we are able to step back without the need to be overly involved emotionally, we are able to deal with much needed matters at hand in a calm and constructive way. This may be emergency restraining of a horse for their own safety in the case of serious injury, to the ability to stand with a horse as he passes, without crying or bombarding him with any form of negative emotion on our part, due to how we may otherwise be feeling.

In instances such as these we are then able to keep our head, keep our breath and heart rate low and safely manage our own energy. This will benefit the horse in question no end, because it is coming from a place of empathy rather than a state of just not caring. It will carry the correct vibration, feel authentic and be of no end of benefit to the horse, enabling them the opportunity to synchronise with our own brain wave state and other physiological functions that will further aid them in maintaining their own calmness in how they deal with their presenting situation.

Imagine a bubble around each individual; each bubble being the energy of their emotions. When we choose to allow that bubble to come into contact with our own and we invade another's emotional energy, it mixes with our own – this is sympathy. We then enable it to distort our own emotional state. The art of empathy however, is when we choose to stand back and observe and read the energy of emotions. We can then see them with clarity. Our own emotional state is intact and we are not distorting the energy of emotions for another individual with our own should a negative mindset prevail within us at any given time.

So for the sake of yourself and the horse whose company you are in please choose to work with empathy over sympathy. They will thank you for it.

I feel it is also important to point out sentience within empathy and how this can cause us to still feel the horse's emotions when we are in the company of a horse, in the same way that they are affected by us through our breath rate, brain wave state and other biological functions. We too will be affected by theirs and this can in many cases cause a change in our own mental and emotional state. This is very different from sympathy and does not automatically mean that it is sympathy that we are experiencing. Rather, this is just a normal physical reaction to the environment that we have found ourselves in. If we are working with empathy then when we remove ourselves from the company of the horse, our body will physically change back to how it was before, as it is no longer synchronising with the biological functions of the horse that is feeling emotionally uncomfortable.

LOOKING GLASS SYNDROME

'Looking Glass Syndrome' is a term I use to explain our perception. The following is a metaphor that I use in order to explain further:

Imagine a dark land, on the land sits a house full of all of the worlds different species. The house has many different windows, each with their own unique differences. Some of the windows will be clear and have beautiful views. Some will only show darkness, some are frosted glass causing distortion and some allow you to see nothing at all. There will also be those that show the view of far away lands, mapping the horizon and allow for the playing out of scenes that we are able to observe and understand. Each one of these scenes will be different; some nice and some not so. Each window and what it has to offer is different for each individual that chooses to stand and stare.

Those in the house will find the window that suits them, the one that enables them to feel the most comfortable. Some may even choose to spend their whole life in that one position, just staring and never venturing to explore or even consider another view. In fact, they may be so static that they are not even aware that another view, another perspective is even possible and exists.

Over time some will choose to move and explore. They will go to the windows of others, enabling them to see not just in their own way, but also as others do. Some may choose to do this only once in their life time, whilst others will make it their role in life to continuously see all points of view - all windows enable them to learn and develop further.

Then we find the truth seeker; the one who has had enough of windows, views and the perceptions of both themselves and others. They believe there to be more to life and they go in search of it. Some may spend years walking around inside the house, only to come across more perceptions, more views. Only one day to find the door that leads them to the great outside. Some may be tentative, even concerned about going outside. Some may stand and wait a while until such a time as they feel ready. Others may grab the door knob and scream 'Thank goodness as I knew there was more to it!'.

When the time is right they will step outside. It may seem dark at first as only too often the distorted or perfectionist view of the windows are incorrect - as seen by those that have ventured outside. As realisation comes and the dark mists start to clear, the veil lifts and truth is now truly observed. No longer is that individual clouded, pulled down and distorted by the vision of others. They now have found the truth in what they seek and are able to see as is truly meant. They close their eyes, give acknowledgment and thanks. They then tip back their head as they open their eyes and they see the sky. 'WOW....this is only the very beginning of the awakening'.

The truth is that not all individuals have the strength of mind to venture outside and some may just be happy within their own perception and their 'lot'. It does not make them bad individuals, nor does it make them stupid. It is just where they are on their life path and within their fragile psyche. It will be dependant on life lessons that they have chosen to reject or to take on board willingly and what their early experiences have both offered and denied them.

The meat eater that declares he loves eating meat will likely never make it out of the house. He will likely never reach the window that offers the slaughterhouse scene. Those that are unable to cope with the death of a loved one will likely never see the sight of the funeral directors back room - they will choose not to venture to that window.

However, when we choose to explore all elevations and all windows, we are able to acknowledge each for what they are. We can do so without having to close our eyes to misery and the plight of others due to an inability to cope with our own emotions. Instead, we will be able to understand how they feel, why they think the way they do and we will be able to find some kind of peace within it. Knowing that is them, we do not need to be like them if we do not choose to be. We can find another perspective and choose to look through the clear windows and then look to the skies for the answers.

No two individuals will be the same; how can they be? Each of their life paths will have offered different life lessons, different circumstances and events. Each of these will have offered them a way to move forwards and even the option to hold back.

The psyche can be fragile; some are already broken beyond repair as shown by our psychiatric words and the sadly disturbed individuals they home, and those that choose to hide in their houses, stable or kennel as the outside world is just too over whelming. Often these are the ones that chose to venture outside too quickly, enabling them to explore too many windows and perceptions first, as well as those forced out with little understanding of others and how and why they do the things that they do to each other - the agoraphobic racing horse; to the abused child and the dog used as bait for fighting dogs.

However, there will be those that know that whatever life has thrown at them - does not have to shape them. They understand that they are not their circumstances or their experiences, but that innately there is more. These are the survivors in life, the ones that choose to heal and can heal to varying degrees by facing their fears, their challenges ahead and wanting to overcome the uncomfortable feeling that exists in the moment. They do this In the full knowledge that life in its entirety is waiting for them. Those individuals are those that I hold the most respect for, those that have found the inner strength to throw caution to the wind - those that feel the fear and do it anyway. These are the warriors of life that will help to bring through a whole new generation of believers in 'self'.

This does not mean for one moment I hold any form of disrespect whatsoever for those that have not ventured outside. Rather, I see where they are in their life and in their own minds, as where they need to be and within their coping with life. But as a truth seeker and having known the journey to get here, I know the struggles and what it entails. Any that choose to tread that path have my greatest respect and support.

EQUINE AUTISM AND LEARNING DIFFICULTIES

Without a doubt horses are complex thinkers; they rely heavily on their senses, not only to communicate with each of us and other horses, but also in order to evaluate their environment and to enable them to keep themselves safe. Through my work as an Animal Communicator and Equine Therapist I have come across some horses that can find their own thought processes problematic and even some that have an absence of a full ability to think and work even simple things out. Many of these horses have problems that may even be best described as 'autistic' in the way in which they often present themselves outwardly.

These developmental issues should not be confused with a break down in communication between horse and care giver. It would be only too easy to assume that our horse doesn't understand even some of the most basic of our requests, through our own lack of ability to communicate clearly and effectively.

Most commonly this is seen in riding where the rider is giving the horse a cue, whilst at the same time giving the horse a conflicting one. This can be caused through lack of experience on the rider's part, as well as a deep seated anxiety that causes our body to give off minute signals that we are totally unaware of. An example of this is tensing our hands when we are holding the reins, which the horse then can feel and then responds to.

Remember everything we say and do around our horse, to them, is information. They then have to interpret this information as best they can and then decide how to react to it. There can be several different causes of learning difficulties in horses. The first one being anxiety. This can cause the horse to over think and this in turn can cause him to constantly think that he hasn't got the request correct, so that he is then left searching for what it is that he thinks you are asking of him. This causes the horse to become more confused to the point that he then finds it hard to think at all, thereby bringing about an ongoing circle of confusion and frustration. This can then be made worse if the rider or handler is not giving the horse a reward or acknowledgment once the correct reaction has been given.

There are also horses that have real learning difficulties and developmental issues, due to biological differences in their brain and how it works. These horses can vary in how badly they are affected. Some may appear mentally switched off and disinterested in any kind of training, whilst others may become easily confused and the result may even be a display of violent behaviour.

There are no hard and fast rules or symptoms as to how these horses appear and react, each of these horses will be different and unique. Nutrition also plays a major role in behaviour and the horses' ability to work things out. Misfiring of the neurotransmitters (brain chemicals) can result in the information being received, but not passed through the brain effectively in a way that it can be used. This can cause the horse to become frustrated and unpredictable as he does not understand what is happening to him. Therefore, once rider and handler error has been ruled out, along with pain and tack issues, deafness or blindness, nutrition should then be the next thing that we look at.

I could not have seen a more perfect example of this than my little Welsh pony a few years ago. He had become very jumpy and unpredictable. He has been on hay, seaweed and a mineral block after a serious infection that had caused major laminitis. When I tested him he showed up as amino acid deficient. I had him blood tested which showed him to be low in protein. I put him on a food named Equine Pure Essentials Base Mix that had a good amount of amino acids/protein in it. Within four to five days his behaviour had completely changed and he was no longer jumpy and became much easier to handle again.

Like us, horses are also very sensitive to atmospheres. It is not uncommon to come across horses that are sensitive to naturally occurring ley lines and other earth energies. As well as peoples moods and approach towards them. Horses don't enjoy feeling frustrated and confused, for them it is not a safe state of mind, nor is it safe for us. This is why it is so important for us to get to the root of the problem. These kinds of behaviours will never be shown by a horse without a cause and it is the cause for each individual horse that we need to find as the causes will all vary. The longer the horse is experiencing stress, then the longer it will be releasing stress chemicals. Over time these stress chemicals will start to affect the physical body and lower the horse's immune system.

If you suspect that your horse is autistic, it is advisable to have your horse assessed by someone that is used to working with such cases. Not only will they be able to help you to rule out other causes, but they will also be able to show you the best way to work with and handle your horse so that the relationship can work. Remember, the more a horse is able to think, the more sensitive the horse and the more emotional intelligence he will have. This is why so many more problems are seen in horses that have above average intelligence. We should never underestimate our horse's ability to think and feel; as when we do, we remove one of the most important ways that we have of understanding the horse's mind and how he feels about the world he has found himself in.

Autism in horses is without a doubt much more common than many would first expect. It is all too easy to label a horse with autism as immature, dangerous, as having learning difficulties, lacking in intelligence or highly strung. In most cases (but by no means all) a horse with autism will be highly intelligent. They will be able to think and see beyond what *we* think we are asking of them and see instead, our true expectations and will instead act upon these. By doing this it would be only too easy through our observations to believe that the horse in question has failed to properly understand our requests, when in actual fact, quite the opposite is correct.

An autistic horse needs clear and precise instruction. All requests need to be very 'black and white' with no areas left unexplained so that there is no way that they can misinterpret our requests. Using traditional methods of training can be very frustrating for these horses, as they tend to question all possibilities of what the instruction we are giving may mean. Hence the need for 'black and white' request and signals. This will avoid them over analysing the request that in most instances will lead to frustration and stress.

When instruction is not given clearly and we hesitate, the horse will become frustrated and may also feel insecure. In such cases, displays of frustration may be exhibited by the horse in the form of undesirable behaviour that is at times violent. The appearance of lack of interest may be seen in quieter personalities. They may show a glazed look in their eye or feel the need to remove themselves from your presence.

As with autism in people, there is a large spectrum on which horses may appear. Ranging from the mild, calm cool character that may well never be discovered and may well just be described as 'stubborn', to the highly strung that is often hard to train with the use of traditional methods and that only a few may have success with. Interestingly unless these horses appear at the more extreme end of the spectrum, their diagnosis may well go undiscovered and in many cases they will go on to lead an almost normal life if they should be lucky enough to find themselves in the right hands.

It should not be forgotten however, that even the calmest and coolest of characters can suffer extreme stress internally, without showing outward symptoms. This can cause these horses to suffer mentally, just as much as those that show their confusion and frustration in their physical behaviour.

At the opposite end of the scale there will be the hypersensitive autistic. These horses will find it hard being in the company of anyone who does not understand their individual needs and level of sensitivity. Chances are they will find day to day life extremely hard and feel as if they are living in a goldfish bowl. Shut off from the outside world as if just observing it without ever feeling part of it. This may also cause them to disconnect and mentally shut down. In many cases this will also lead to the forming of 'vices' as a coping mechanism.

A horse with autism can go on to lead a wonderful and fulfilling life when placed in the right environment and with the correct training. More often than not, people with autism and those with the ability to think 'outside of the box' will make the best caregivers for these horses.

Horses with autism can understandably cause huge frustration for people who do not understand their needs and how they learn. It is not unusual for these horses to be beaten for their behaviour. The highly strung horse will sometimes choose to retaliate whilst in many cases both they and the calmer personalities will just take the violence aimed towards them. These horses will never take their eye off of their abuser whilst that abuse is taking place. Without a doubt, horses with autism are 'truth seekers' by nature and due to this will always seek out and feel most at home with those that stand in their own truth.

Several years ago I was contacted by an Equine Chiropractor that had taken on a horse that had been labelled as violent. After engaging in horse communication with him, it became apparent that his was a typical case of autism. I explained this to his owner and did my best to explain a way forwards for them. His owner (and rightly so) felt it important that she definitively rule out all other possible causes for his behaviour. Four thousand pounds worth of tests later, the diagnosis by the Vet was given as autism. As it turned out the owner had not told the Vet what my suspicions were, this was a diagnosis that they came to themselves based on the tests and presenting symptoms that were being exhibited.

To my knowledge this is the first veterinary diagnosis of a horse with autism in the UK, though of course there may have been many since or those that I have not been aware of. For me this is a massive break through in the recognition of autism in horses and enabling them to be properly understood.

Currently living in my herd I have a little black Arabian by the name of Manta. He shows obvious symptoms of both autism and learning difficulties. His reactions to other horses and his body language with them on the surface may appear normal, but on close observation it is easy to see that he can sometimes struggle to find a correct response. This is far more clearly seen when he interacts with people. Even the most simple request for something that he knows how to do can become over whelming for him. His coping mechanism for this is to simply walk away which we always let him do.

One day a few years ago, Manta escaped from his field. He took himself for a walk up our driveway towards a dead end. Usually when a horse escapes in this way they will become excited (in this instance new green grass was on offer). I called out to Manta using his name but he just continued to walk. I managed to catch up with him and again I was ignored and he just kept walking forwards without acknowledging me at all. Usually when we catch up with an escaped horse, or we go in pursuit of them, they will do one of two things. They will either run off displaying excitement, or they will stop when asked. As no acknowledgment of my request to stop was forth coming, I gently put my hand out and touched his chest and again asked Manta to stop, again I was ignored and he showed no signs at all of response.

At no time did Manta look at me, acknowledge my presence in anyway or even change his walking speed. Once Manta got to the dead end, he just stopped and stood quietly for me to put his head collar on and I was able to lead him back safely to his field.

This is pretty typical behaviour for Manta. It is not that he is not listening to you, but that sometimes he retreats into his own little world and is literally unable to mentally hear you. Due to his gentle handling and natural life style he is able to cope well and we ask nothing of him that he is unable to offer.

Although Manta is able to associate a few words with simple requests, for instance he understands that the word 'leg' is a request to lift his leg. He appears unable to associate a certain word, his name, with himself. When I am doing groundwork with my other horses or when one of them is having a therapy session, Manta will always stand as close to us as he can. We can see that he is wanting to engage with us and that he wants to be part of it, but that sadly he is unable to. The moment he is invited to take part, no matter how subtly, he immediately becomes more alert and more often than not he will walk away. Manta also struggles with eye contact from people. Looking him in the eye or even focusing your gaze on his face can make him feel extremely uncomfortable.

EQUINE MENTAL ILLNESS

As horses have all of the same Neuro-peptides (emotional chemicals) not only in their brain but also in every organ of their body, as we do, it is only too easy to understand how so many of our horses, due to hereditary issues, environmental, work and owner issues, are suffering from mental health in our hands today. Equine mental illness is something that many horse owners and trainers alike do not have a full understanding of. Whilst some may describe a horse as 'switched off', depressed and anxious, due to not using correct labelling and terms for these disorders, much of the seriousness of the horse's mental state falls by the wayside.

Couple this with the fact that it is so often people, owners and trainers, that are causing much of the horses mental illnesses that we see today and it is no wonder why the alarm bells to not ring for many. All too often when someone has an anxious horse their primary concern will be that it is 'highly strung', will not stand still, is flighty and is generally a pain in the backside to ride and he is not listening or focused. How many people consider the fact that this same horse maybe suffering from Post Traumatic Stress Disorder (PTSD) due to their past? Hmmm...when you give it that title it kind of brings the full complexity of the issue into focus does it not?

The bottom line is that there is no reason why a horse can not suffer from the same mood altering states and mental illnesses that humans do.

It would be exceptionally hard for me to write a list that covers all of the symptoms that may be displayed by the horse. This is due to the fact that basically every single action, symptom and mannerism that the horse displays could in fact be a typical symptom of mental illness - other than calm, grounded quiet. The danger comes when two or more of these symptoms are very apparent in their nature, or three or more lesser symptoms are seen together. If we see this being exhibited by the horse, we can take this as a danger sign that there is something a miss that needs looking into.

Sadly as horses are unable to sit on a therapists couch or lie on the vets table whilst discussing their inner most thoughts with them, it can be hard for a vet to be able to make a clinical diagnosis other than what is being seen by way of physical symptoms. These are the same type of symptoms that will also be seen whilst the horse is in pain, or has another type of health issue. For instance: A deficiency of vitamin E can cause a horse to feel run down and cause him to lack energy. This kind of lethargy could easily be mistaken for a horse that is just 'having a tired day', too much work has been expected from him or he is fed up over the weather. He could in fact be suffering from depression due to a lack of sunlight, an ill fitting rug, being shut in his stable for prolonged periods of time as well as being vitamin D deficient. So there we have a classic case of a horse that is suffering from a nutritional issue that due to external and environmental factors as well as diet is suffering from mental illness - and a physical one which both show the same kind of symptoms.

How often have we heard people say 'My horse loves being in his stable, sometimes he doesn't even want to come out of it!' - Hmmm!

The horse is a prey animal, he would not choose to lock himself in a stable given the choice. It is us as humans that have created this habit and false environment for him. Forced incarceration, coupled with a lack of stimulation and exercise can all lead to feelings of agoraphobia (fear of large outside spaces) and forced incarceration syndrome causing (in some cases) horses to fear stepping outside of their stable for varying periods of time. This is something that *we* have created. The horse was not the one who locked himself in and deprived himself of his needs.

Of course it is also fair to say that some horses genuinely do like to spend sometime in their stables. It gives them time to get out of bad weather, to not have to worry that another herd member will pinch their food and gives them time to lie down and rest on a soft, dry bed. It is when there is a precursor there for the development of it becoming a mental illness that we have to be careful.

There is so much I could write about equine mental illness that it would literally be a book in itself. For this reason rather than to write that book now - I will instead, now that the seed has been planted, leave you with some information regarding the various different types of illnesses that our horses can suffer from.

Anxiety Disorders

This may be seen as an over reaction to an object or a situation over which the horse feels that he has no control over. If this is seen we need to ask the following questions:

Does the horse have any control or influence over his reactions?

Does his anxiety have an effect over his normal everyday functioning?

Is his response (as a prey animal) over the object or situation appropriate?

Is his anxiety response only seen during times of certain phobias or in certain company?

Does he sweat?

Does his heartbeat increase?

Mood Disorders

Does his personality fluctuate between different ends of the scale, for example: Periods of feeling extreme sadness and lethargy to periods of extreme excitement and being overly mentally stimulated. Once he is 'stuck' in one type of mood, how easily is he able to rid himself of it and find balance in feeling content?

Impulse Control and Addiction Disorders

A horse that is suffering from this disorder will likely be unable to control his impulses and actions that may in some cases cause both him and others harm. This can often be seen in horses that are possessive over their food to the point that they will kick out and bite, even if there is no immediate threat that it will be taken from them. The food bowl just equals uncontrollable impulsive reaction for them.

Personality Disorders

Sufferers will often exhibit inflexible behaviours and intolerance towards others. This may be seen as the horse that likes you one minute and attacks you or another herd member the next. There will be no obvious reason for his flitting between two personalities and it will be totally beyond his control. He will literally just react according to how he feels at that moment.

Obsessive Compulsive Disorder (OCD)

Box walking, weaving, stable door banging, windsucking and cribbing will all fall into this category. Whilst there may be an underlying desire to create these behaviours due to the fact that they also release endorphins, such behaviours will also be compulsive in nature as to the fact the horse may have little control over being able to stop himself from doing them.

Post Traumatic Stress Disorder (PTSD)

The precursor for this disorder will likely be something such as an accident, abuse, a change of home, loss of a best friend - whether they be human or horse, or an event that has otherwise been tragic and deeply emotional for them. A horse suffering from post traumatic stress disorder will find that they reach extreme anxiety levels very quickly. For some an experience need only be similar to the original trauma for the mind to go into overdrive and the body to react in a stressful manner.

When we put our horses, as well as their emotions and behaviours into the context that we have above with their correct titles and explanations, it is only too easy to see just what a raw deal our horse's get in the hands of humans. If they were human, these horses would of course be getting treatment for their emotional disorders. They would in some cases be medicated, offered therapy and they would have someone help them to look at their life style and environment, as well as how they think that would help them to make changes and acceptance where needed. Not only do most of our horses not get this help, their actions are just put down to 'behaviour' and they are often punished for it. Unacceptable? Yes totally! But such is the way of the equestrian world today - how deeply sad.

NEONATAL MALADJUSTMENT SYNDROME

As I do not breed horses I had not heard of this issue before. However, having stumbled across Xas's story, her owner Camille was only to happy to share it with us all being as it is such an important one. I made the decision to keep the story in its entirety, rather than editing it down. As I felt it important that we were able to follow Xas through her years to see both the positive changes and the challenges that she has had to face.

My interest in her story is also founded in the fact that much of what is described within it, very much resonates with me, on a personal level. Whilst I am not party to the knowledge as to whether one of my own horses was in fact born with this syndrome, there is without a doubt numerous similarities to what I have observed with him in the last twelve years since he came to me as a yearling.

Horses born with 'Dummy Foal Syndrome' are given this title due to the dummy like symptoms they display. They may also be tilted, wanderers, barkers or sleepers.

It is thought that the tissues of the brain haemorrhage causes swelling around the nerve cells due to oedema. Haemorrhage may result from low or high oxygen surges in the blood that then circulate through the brain. In some cases seizures will be seen in foals that are affected, or they may suffer from a lack of correct suckling response.

The blood/brain barrier in a foal develops over a period of several weeks after birth. This means that should the foal contract an infection during this time, it is possible that the infection may breach the immature barrier and make its way into the brain.

'Dummy foal' is one of the terms used to describe NMS, Neonatal Maladjustment Syndrome. Despite the apparent severity of the symptoms at birth, the long-term prognosis is said to be good for those foals who survive. Xas was a survivor and her story tells how in fact the challenges that horses face, are no different from those of people who live with any level of brain-damage.

I will now hand you over to Camille Dareau in order that she can relay Xas's story to you and the challenges faced by this mare and battles that she won - against the odds.

Origins Of A Dummy Foal

Xas was the first foal we bred; a pure thoroughbred.

Her dam-sire is Java Tiger who is a big grey racehorse who was known for his ability to sire competition horses, and for stamping his distinctive colour. Xas's sire was a racehorse called Captain Maverick who was bred in the United States. Although he was by the famous French stallion Nureyev, he himself was less successful on the racecourse, due to this he ended up covering heavier mares to produce horses for show jumping and only the occasional racehorse. As Dummy Foal syndrome affects mostly thoroughbred foals, it was probably the narrow gene pool of Xas's lineage that is partly responsible for her problems at birth.

Xas's mother Tiggy, was a living example of the many mistakes people make with horses. She had been race-trained, but she had never made the racecourse. When we bought her as a four year old, her digestive system was already badly damaged due to the cereal rich, low forage diet that she had been on. Her feet had sand-cracks which had not yet opened right up, but her hooves were soft and flat and she had already been shod for several years. She was a fairly timid mare but she had developed a hard, stubborn side as a way of protecting herself from demands that she was unable to cope with.

For many years she had serious problems with red-worm infection. At the time we were following the conventional opinion in most areas of horse-management, so we probably half killed her with synthetic wormers, which never made much difference to the worms. We tried to fix her feet with egg-bar shoes and metal plates. In her training she was perpetually lazy and any instruction I resorted to, would result in me having to force her. Any prolonged period of work seemed to result in her injuring herself in some way, probably in order to ensure a sufficient recovery time! She spent more time 'resting' than she ever did working.

We had ups and downs - mostly downs, although we were learning. By the time we eventually lost her to melanomas which were beginning to influence her quality of life too much, she had a lovely last summer here in France, her feet were healed and she had at last enjoyed some gentle work.

In a world where people do the 'right thing' we would never have bred from Tiggy of course. She had not proved herself in competition, and she had too many health issues. That world misses the point though and Tiggy's babies have both been priceless teachers, as well as giving Tiggy herself something back to compensate for all the mistakes we made with her along the line.

Discovering Dummy Foal Syndrome

This is an extract from my diary at the time, written in the middle of May in 1999. It describes the first stressful days of Xas's life.

"Tiggy had her baby at some time between 2.30 and 4.30am on Thursday morning. When I went out in the morning at about 4.30am, I walked round the field in the mist and I found her standing at the edge of the reeds, then I saw some dark ears flickering - it was amazing to realise she'd had her baby. When I moved closer I saw the foal was the kind of brown colour that turns into grey eventually. I saw that she was a filly a bit later on, so in many ways a miniature Tiggy. She was struggling to get up and not managing at all really, so I milked off a bit of colostrum and gave it to her from the bottle - I then went to get help. With Gaby's help we got the filly standing, but Tiggy didn't want to let her out of her sight to suckle, also Tiggy's bag was very tight and she (Xas) couldn't seem to get to the teats.

When I look back now I can see all of the mistakes, but also I don't think that those mistakes caused the problem. They were just inadequate responses. We should have called the vet out then, but I didn't really realise she wasn't a normal foal. We left her for a bit after giving her more colostrum. It was a bit chilly too because of the mist. She did get up by herself again, but she couldn't manage to suckle. Then the situation got worse and worse, Tiggy got very difficult to milk and we were trying to strip her so the foal could suckle and the foal was getting weaker. The vet was on his way when she started to behave in a particularly abnormal fashion - as if she had brain damage. We took them in - with the foal in a wheelbarrow and poor Tiggy was quite wound up. She (Xas) was very ill when we got her into the stable, she was curled up and unable to stand - she was shivering. The vet didn't think she had any chance of survival.

Back to my Diary

"So we began a long and exhausting process, but slowly things have shaped up. I felt then that way I always feel - that I had faith in the process of healing. She [Xas] was tubed with the milk we were able to get, we also got her onto drips and plasma. She was wrapped up in rugs and we had to hold her through the convulsions. Tiggy was very difficult to milk, she was sedated twice - we got straw in to bed up the box and lambs teats (rubber) for later if she would suckle. All of that night we had her on the drips until midday Friday. She was starting to fill-in and become soft and full of fluid, I was also treating her a bit [with Cranio-Sacral Therapy] and her cranium was very distressed. Her O-A [Occipito-Atlantal junction] was also jammed pretty solid - in fact, I sensed that was the real problem. In the morning she was getting very strong and the vet came with more drips to take her through to twelve - that was the worst time and it was seriously exhausting. [Thankfully, during this marathon our friends Fiona and Patrick generously offered their help so that we could get some rest!]. It was such a relief when the drip was finished and we could let her go and she was now starting to drink more. Her suckling reflex was good through the night. When we let her go she actually walked around with a normal head carriage - with no sign of an issue except a slight tip you could only see when viewing her from the front."

"It was incredible. I knew she would live then - although I always really knew. For the rest of the Friday she was drinking more and more with each feed. Every 15 minutes at first and then every half an hour until eventually every hour later in the night. She took the bottle lying down most of the time it was offered to her and Tiggy had really started to relax and accept the syringe milking. By the Saturday night, Xas was getting up more easily and was starting to investigate Tiggy. We put the rubber teat over Tiggy's teat to introduce her to standing the right way, but we didn't really try to force her to suckle yet, it was still too early for her. As it turned out we never actually had to because she got stronger and stronger. By twelve on Sunday she was suckling by herself! It was fantastic because before she was unable to attach and then when she could, she didn't actually suckle.

In the middle of Saturday I treated her quite a lot and so she had then slept a lot and seemed very tired, but the healing work cleared so much. On Sunday I didn't feel she could cope with more until the evening - there is quite a fixed kind of pattern, inherent in a way, through the Cervicals - that suggests she lay that way in the womb - developed that way maybe? I don't know, but it clears more every time. She still has a badly bruised left eye where she bashed it on the wall on Thursday.

On Sunday, after she was suckling on her own, we put them out in the glebe [the little meadow behind our house]. Tiggy trotted around very energetically with her baby cantering along like a tumbleweed at her side. Since then they have really bonded and we can leave them much more to themselves. She is suckling very frequently and enjoying it very much. Now it's just her eye and the trace of a tilt...that is remaining".

Following Wednesday... "she is going out into the field, she is playing and she is being quite independent. She is growing strong now. Every evening when she comes in, she lies down and stretches out and expects a treatment!

Growing Up With Dummy Foal Syndrome

The title of this section is deliberate, because although Xas became an apparently normal foal, doing all the foal things such as jumping out of her field twice in the first month and hassling the older gelding she befriended endlessly - she was not a normal foal. Her brain damage has affected her in certain ways throughout her entire life and working with her has been particularly educational due of that. For example, in a normal growth process, the rates of growth of the different structures are harmonised by our innate life intelligence. In Xas's case some processes were a little out of sync. For her first three years, every autumn she had a mystery lameness. The pedal bone seemed to be out of alignment and her tendons were rock hard. I realised at some point that her bones were simply growing faster than her tendons and ligaments. Eventually when she reached her adult size she stabilised.

Having been a dummy foal also gave her certain advantages in comparison with the other horses. For example, her spatial awareness is exceptional in most circumstances - she can feel instantly what is under her feet (someone's foot for example!).

On the other hand, in her early years she had little instinct for self preservation. Her inability to judge objects or situations external to her, landed her in trouble more than once. She somehow caught herself up in the hay feeder when she was a yearling so that each leg was trapped inside. Incredibly she only sustained a slight swelling on the bone of one fetlock joint, although in recent years that has enlarged somewhat. She also tangled herself in electric fencing and got a bad burn on her hock which took over a month to heal.

It is true that sometimes she gives the impression of being perhaps a little retarded. For example, she has always needed a 'helper' to look after her when she eats outside, otherwise she is likely to throw her food bowl around or scatter food everywhere. In fact, a horse-whisperer who once communicated with her described her as autistic, which would make sense after the dummy foal syndrome. Interestingly she said that the parts of Xas's brain that were damaged related to short term memory and reasoning powers. It is true that she is a very accepting and laid back horse considering her experiences, which perhaps makes sense if she doesn't remember things for very long.

On the other hand, as she has matured she seems to have developed a particularly good reasoning ability. One day whilst we were out riding, we were trying to decide whether to go over a little bridge instead of through the stream. Xas took one look at it and instantly strode through the stream without a hesitation. She is also aware of 'problems' and she puzzles them out in an unhorse-like way.

The example of this that I remember most clearly happened not long after we moved to France. Xas was five or six years old and her younger sister Cava, kept breaking out of their field into the woods at the back of the farm. One time she got stuck and this was the last straw for Xas. She was preoccupied all of that day when she was in her stable. That night returning to the field she seemed different; like someone who has a plan. When we reached the top of the road, she turned left instead of carrying on as we usually would and took me without any hesitation, straight to the field which has the most secure fencing. It was so funny that I had to follow her advice. Once Ca-va and her were safely installed, there was a definite look of relief on her face - as well as a touch of pride in her problem-solving ability.

The other horses have always accepted her 100% and in a kind of special way as if they could sense her dummy foal differences and they never showed any signs of rejecting her. As she has matured, she has become the 'supervisor', or the 'maternal one'. One morning it was very frosty and the ground was slippery. We had recently 'rescued' an ex-racehorse from the local horse fair and she was still not used to negotiating such terrain. Xas understood this and put herself in front of Odette, making her walk extremely slowly all of the way in, even strictly preventing the little 'race' to get into the stables at the end that had become Odette's particular naughty habit.

How would Dummy Foal Syndrome Affect Her Early work?

Looking at Xas's life with hindsight, it is possible to see the cycles she has made every year. Like the cycles of a spiral, she always came back round to the same issues, but she reached higher and pushed further towards physical strength, suppleness and wholeness in her nervous system each time around.

In her third year, at the beginning of lunging work, she started to show some mild signs of head-shaking. Many horses with head-shaking symptoms will often have restriction patterns in their cervical (neck) vertebrae and this was certainly one of Xas's weak points. Possibly even a root cause of her dummy foal syndrome, due to influence on her spinal cord.

In Xas's case, some basic Cranio-Sacral work was enough to give the nerves enough clearance and she never showed head-shaking signs again throughout her adult life. Except during a period much later on, when she was mainly hacking out and she would start to shake her head after some work on the contact. This could have been soreness when her neck muscles became tired, or the result of bruising in her mouth from a blind wolf tooth. Our horse dentist had just started taking them out, because he suspected they were sometimes causing a problem. Either her neck strengthened up, or her mouth became comfortable because the shaking resolved itself in time.

The most obvious influence of the Dummy Foal Syndrome at that time was her extremely short attention span and the way things could get too much for her very easily. One distraction too many would cause her to explode. She could only really work for a few minutes at first, building up very gradually to a twenty minute session and never more than half an hour, up until well into her fourth year.

It was always a case of keeping her calm enough to be able to relax enough physically to find her coordination and become supple, all before she lost her focus because she became too stressed physically in her brain.

She always wanted to stretch her neck right down and hold her head very low to the ground at a certain point in the session, she still does now. This was obviously connected to oxygen imbalance in her brain, as a result of the Dummy Foal Syndrome, but I was never really sure if it was too much or too little going through. I never pushed her beyond this point as she tended to need enough time in between sessions to recuperate and develop herself. Definitely more than most horses.

Immediately after her recovery from the Dummy Foal Syndrome, her paces seemed normal, but later on tightness had started to creep in as a result of her unbalanced growing phases, as well as a marked lack of coordination in canter, especially the left rein. She would disunite or move in a four beat canter. I found the best solution was pole-work and little jumps, not only did she enjoy that, but it purified her strides and her central nervous system patterning developed in the right direction. Her trot-work gradually transformed into a cadenced, open movement.

She was just at the point of walking around quietly with a rider, giving that lovely safe feeling some horses seem to, when Xas had another crisis. It was literally a few weeks before we were packing up all thirteen horses and moving to France. It was a lameness again, but didn't seem to have any direct relation to the Dummy Foal Syndrome. She was unable to use one of her hind legs and she gradually worsened day by day. By this time I was well on the way to turning away from conventional treatment, although this one was a scary test. I gave her homeopathic and herbal painkillers and took time to distance myself from the doubt and fearfulness which creates a smokescreen in front of what is actually going on. I wasn't experienced enough at the time to feel what I know now was a massive traveling abscess in the entire limb, moving up as far as the sacroiliac joint. But I could feel the power of the process and so I did what I could to support it. After a few days of fever and intense pain, her system won out and she was walking again. By the time it came to go in the lorry to France, she strode up the ramp like she had been traveling all of her life. I suspect there was a significant emotional element to her latest crisis, worrying about the move and what was involved, but she fought it off and rose to the challenge.

About a month later in France, the whole sole of the foot of that leg came off, and we could see the enormity of the abscess that had been underneath.

I believe when we are healthy enough, our bodies clear out toxins in these ways, sometimes in abscesses or cysts. Xas had been injected with plenty of drugs when she had the Dummy Foal Syndrome. Maybe the herbs and therapy she had since that time had helped her to purify her system in this radical way?

Two steps forward, five steps back

Xas was making great progress once we arrived and she had settled in France well. Although she found the general brightness and greenness of everything fascinating and a bit overwhelming. The Dummy Foal Syndrome had definitely affected her perception of colour and different surfaces, but she was rarely scared of anything. I was taking her on short little hacks so she could become acclimatised to the aids very slowly. She was very sensitive to the balance of her rider, but she had inherited her mother's suspicion of anyone trying to take advantage of her.

One day I had an argument with her about how she was accepting the contact, I didn't try to fiddle with her mouth in any way, but by trying to make her loosen her neck from my seat and leg, I forced her boundaries because I didn't back off when she got tense about it. I was annoyed with myself for a lot longer than she was, but it helped me to realise that another consequence of the Dummy Foal Syndrome, was that in every different scenario, she was a completely different horse. I had assumed that the self carriage she had been learning in the arena would be there in her central nervous system on a hack. This was not the case at all, whatever part of her that assimilated and developed this posture was only accessible in the arena. There is always an element of distraction with any horse hacking out, but in her case, she was a different horse and she had to go through the whole process again - separately when hacking out. We alternated between arena work and hacking out in an attempt to integrate but it made no apparent difference. The more her training has progressed however, the better she has holistically harmonised.

Working with Xas was a bit like having to use all of the roads in the whole country to get to the other side. There are no real shortcuts with horses anyway, but the Dummy Foal Syndrome seemed to have unraveled her consciousness like knitting - right back to the basics. By being patient and having no expectations from one day to the next and seeing every step forward as a bonus, it was and still is a great opportunity to see how things are actually worked out in a horse's mind and body, step by step.

Maybe Xas felt she needed a bit of time out at this point in her life, but at the end of the summer - seemingly always a dangerous time for her - she was kicked by another horse. It was a freak accident, a tiny bit of horn from the other mare's hoof was lodged under her skin, causing the whole of the back of her leg to open up so the foreign object could be ejected. What followed was over nine months of hell.

Whether it was because her healing systems were a bit slow because of the Dummy Foal Syndrome, or just the nature of the wound being where the tight skin is at the back of the canon bone, it grew proud flesh like crazy. At the end of January the following year she had to be operated on in order to remove it. We used an ointment we found from the United States called Equaide to help with healing the vast wound she had after the surgery. Thankfully it did an amazing job, as we were beginning to lose hope that she would ever heal. The vet said she would never be rideable again and certainly never become sound because of the scarring on the tendon.

This kind of prognosis has never really worried us - after all, if we had listened to the Vet in Scotland we would have lost her to the Dummy Foal Syndrome at the start. We simply saw it as a bonus that she was still with us and doing so well.

She went out with the other horses as soon as the wound was reasonably healed. We walked her up our steep hill every day to help the tendon to re-pattern as before and to avoid the development of adhesions. By the summer she was back in work. We did enough careful lunging to build her top-line back up and by the next year she was ready to go into the next phase of her education.

Back to Work

That summer we had several working students for all but the most tricky of our horses. Although it was never possible to bully Xas, she has always been very sensible and honest. She was an excellent teacher because she had to be melted and formed, gently and respectfully and success meant an opportunity to feel her considerable power.

Around that time we were working with a very good Osteopath. Dorothée Breton was particularly sensitive and we found that some horses found the Osteopathic approach less intimidating than the Cranio-Sacral Therapy, also that the CST was very important for integrating any spinal or pelvic manipulations. Dorothée looked at Xas and said that one of the vertebrae at the top of her neck was actually deformed and much smaller than normal. She didn't think it would be safe to manipulate it, but she did think that the work Xas was doing was helping her as the muscle was able to support her.

Correct engagement gradually supples all of the horse's joints, including vertebral ones. Of course I wondered how much of a part the deformity had played in her developing Dummy Foal Syndrome at birth. It was another reason to be 'thankful' we had never used any kind of auxiliary aid or physical force to make her 'come round'. Who knows what kind of damage could have been done?

She was really beginning to think she could be a dressage horse now, the aids were making sense to her and she was able to truly engage for the first time. She seemed to be able to transcend her body, although she found it hard to raise her neck into a more advanced posture. It had always seemed after those first terrible Dummy Foal days that anything at all was a bonus, but now she was progressing so well it was exciting to think that maybe it could be possible that all that power she promised might actually fulfill its potential.

The Home Run, From Dummy Foal to Queen Of the Herd

Ever since I treated Xas in the early days for the Dummy Foal Syndrome, I could feel I had to be careful. I couldn't treat her brain itself for many years, too much change in her system could bring on a brief healing crisis. Sometimes she would have pain in her neck and lie down and want to jam herself up against the stable walls. The Cranio-Sacral Therapy was the only thing which could bring her out of it, but it had to be done with care. These episodes seemed to take place once or twice a year, lasting a few hours, maybe longer. It would have seemed very bizarre if we had not understood her history of course.

The summer after her working student time however, she entered a crisis which was much more critical than usual. It seemed to be the heat in the summer which was affecting her at first, she stopped eating very much, she lay down a lot and she had a slight temperature. We gave her large volumes of colloidal silver in case it was some kind of infection, but I knew it was not a disease as such, it was almost as if her system had reached the make or break point. Either her body would change to allow her to achieve what she wanted to do or it wouldn't - there was no middle ground.

For what seemed like weeks she was on and off and she lost a lot of condition. At this time we had a working student, Naomi Sharp, staying with us who was discovering her ability to communicate with the horses in terms of their thoughts. We had been doing some great 'double' treatments, reaching the horses minds and bodies at the same time.

When we did this with Xas there were many physical and emotional issues which she wanted to address. One of the fundamental issues to emerge was that she didn't want me to feel responsible for her anymore because she was handicapped or defective. She wanted to be the responsible one. Not only responsible for herself either, she wanted to look after us now and she no longer wanted to be seen as 'special needs'. Physical things such as a lack of development in her intestine as a result of the Dummy Foal Syndrome and patterns from further back which had influenced how her neck had developed, were also addressed during the treatment.

After the treatment her appetite came back and she gradually began to put weight back on. For the next six months she seemed to be undergoing what felt like a complete spinal reconstruction, even in the spinal cord itself.

Other changes began to happen. Whereas she had always been accepted in the herd and got on with other horses, as an adult, Xas had never really been a participator. Maybe the Dummy Foal Syndrome had made her feel too heavy and slow in her head to want to join in much, or have profound relationships with the others. The new Xas simply took her chosen place in the herd, right at the top.

She started to develop a close relationship with Phoenix, the most dominant gelding, and now they are rarely apart. The herd began to follow her when she chose to go somewhere and trusted her decisions. She became a genuine passive leader; instead of dominating the other horses she was confident in herself and her decisions and she inspired the same confidence in the others. Especially Phoenix who has been severely traumatised in the past.

In terms of her training, more of the story has been revealing itself and I understand more now about how the Dummy Foal Syndrome affects her. Recently I realised that she controls the oxygen reaching her brain by holding her diaphragm. Releasing the horse's diaphragm is one of the main portals to engagement. It allows the rider's leg to merge with the horse and bringing both postural systems into alignment, but for Xas, it is also exposing her brain to change. This is why it is so important that I respect her boundaries; only she knows how much she can let go. The more she 'lets go', the straighter and more energetically she can move and ultimately, the healthier she becomes. It would appear that her brain has to be able to accommodate the level of change. This is why it is a profound test of our trust in each other.

When I ride her now, I think of it like a journey to find water. At first I am crawling through a tunnel which is dry and narrow and the progress is slow. Gradually I am easing my way through and there seems to be a bit more room and the walls are smoother. Soon I am finding a little stream of water here and there. I can hear a waterfall in the distance, incredibly powerful, but I can't reach it straight away. I have to be patient and believe that I will find it. Some days I do find it and it is magical.

THE HORSE IN PAIN

A horse that is experiencing pain is to a large degree a little in the dark. Other than through carrying out what are often felt to be invasive tests, it can be hard to not only locate where the pain is originating from, but also to what level it is being experienced.

Being as horses, like humans, have varyingly different pain thresholds, two horses with the same pain levels may present outwardly as being very different. Whilst the horse that has a low threshold for pain maybe on three legs with a serious limp due to lameness, the horse with the same degree of pain but a higher tolerance for it, may still be walking on all four legs with just a slight limp being seen. It is often the case that when a horse experiences prolonged and chronic pain, that they will have found a way to cope to a certain degree and they will be seen to 'get on with it' and 'work through it'. The danger here is that if the cause of the pain is injury, the horse may further cause damage to himself through his willingness to still weigh bare and maybe even still work. This may be also seen in cases of acute injury where adrenalin and endorphins come into play which cause the horse to not at first feel the full intensity of the pain and damage.

If I had a pound for every time I had heard someway say that their horse is not experiencing any pain when they were, I would have been able to retire years ago! The least amount of areas that I have ever found to be sore in a horse was three. This was a three year old horse that belonged to an Equine Physiotherapist.

Being as horses are not symmetrical, there will be a degree of natural crookedness that horses will have and then have to compensate for. Over a period of time this may result in shortening of tendons and tightening of certain muscles as a way to keep the rest of their body balanced and sound.

How the individual horse's pain receptors send out pain signals and works with the horse's nervous system will also have a huge effect on how differently horses experience pain. A Physiotherapist once offered a good analogy for explaining this:

When we have long term pain the nervous system will form a pattern of signals that it continues to send out. Over time as the signals keep travelling along this path it will start to become a dirt track. Should the cause of the pain then not be dealt with and the signals continue to be sent out. They then start to widen the dirt track, until over time a full blown motorway is created. This then allows the pain signals to have a free rein to keep travelling at a fast and clear rate.

So in other words, the longer pain goes on, the more the brain gets used to sending out the signals, so the brain continues to send them, due to a now confused brain and nervous system. Further to this the brain creates a map of that pain. The pain brain map may then choose to continue sending out those signals even if the injury, or the otherwise physical issue heals, until such a time as the map for that issue is altered.

There are two main groups of pain:

Nociceptive Pain

This type of pain occurs usually due to injury or damage to the tissues. It causes the nerve endings in the affected area to become activated or damaged which causes them to send pain signals to the brain. To some degree this type of pain, if only experienced for a short time, can be the horse's friend. Whilst pain is not nice to experience and we do not want to see our horse in pain. Nociceptive pain can stop a horse from trying to walk on a badly injured leg, or cause him to lift his foot quickly off of a sharp stone before it gets the chance to badly bruise his sole. It plays a vital role in being a voice for the body in order to alert the horse that there is a physical issue that needs to be attended to. Imagine if no pain was felt at all by the horse, just how many injuries and near fatal ones would he have and all because he couldn't feel pain? He could stand with his barrel against an electric fence whilst he slept and the tape burnt into his skin and flesh. He could engage in fights with other horses to the death, as he felt no pain to cause him to retreat. In many ways pain is the horses' friend, dependent on which form it comes in and how long it stays and if it is proportional to the presenting physical issue.

Neuropathic Pain

This type of pain is nerve pain. It is seen in cases of both neuralgia and trigeminal pain. More often than not, the way the pain is experienced will be different from nociceptive pain, although both types of pain may also be experienced together. Neuropathic pain is usually experienced as burning sensations, as well as sharp and sudden stabbing and electric shock type pains. Symptoms of neuropathic pain can come in many different forms:

A sudden buck, rear or kick

Refusal to have bridle or head collar put on

Head shy

Rubbing face on leg or fencing

Unusually quite and withdrawn demeanour

Withdrawing from the rest of the herd and standing alone

Loss of appetite

'Gone feral'

Neuropathic pain in many instances can be hard to diagnose as it will sometimes be intermittent. Further to this other than the horse's reactions to the pain (the symptoms of which may be indicative of other issues also) there maybe nothing presenting physically, for instance, no injury sight or misalignment.

Around eight years ago I received a call from a lady whose horse had been in hospital for two weeks. Extensive tests had been carried out in order to try and find the cause of her horse not being able to move correctly, or put his head down to graze. All that the tests had come up with was an arthritic joint in his neck that was not bad enough, or of the correct nature to be able to cause the presenting physical issues. I was able to locate a masked pain in the horse's wither on his right side. ('Masked pain' is the term I use to describe a pain that when touched or manipulated, does not feel any worse so produces no outward reaction from the horse). Arrangements were made for myself and an Osteopath to visit the horse in order to see what could be done to help him. The Osteopath that I chose is one that works similarly to myself, as in he is able to locate pain and other issues that are not visible to the naked eye. Locating the issue on an intuitive, feeling level, rather than through observation and symptom based diagnosis. This enabled treatment to go a head, the result being a horse that was afterwards able to move correctly and lower his head to graze.

Around five years ago my little pony Meeka started to show symptoms of neuropathic trigeminal pain. She would refuse to have a head collar on, would stand with her backend facing the fence and would periodically kick out. Although naturally by nature a quiet pony, she has also started to stand alone in the field shelter, away from the other herd members which was unlike her normal behaviour. These were all sure symptoms that she was experiencing a pain issue. An Osteopath was called out and her trigeminal nerve was treated with laser therapy. In only the space of a few minutes, her pain was gone. Sadly Meeka also had Cushings Syndrome and a brain tumour so it was not long after that she was put to sleep.

Trigeminal pain and often neuropathic pain in general is often referred to as the 'suicide pain'. The level and intensity of this type of pain may vary, but in cases where it is high level and incessant, it has literally driven some people to commit suicide.

How many horses are out there with this level and type of pain?

How many of them are being labelled 'grumpy' and 'uncooperative'?

How many are not working correctly because they physically 'can't' due to the disruption of their nervous system and their neurotransmitters incorrectly firing that stop their correct muscular responses?

How many are not working correctly due to an inability to focus due to their pain levels?

How many owners are forcing the issue over bridling and head collars as their horse is being 'naughty'?

One of the other issues relating to nerve pain that I come across quite often in horses, is issues with their teeth. Some horses will have a degree of nerve pain in one or more teeth, but not enough to stop them eating. Sometimes it is not until such a time as a metal bit touches those teeth, bangs against them or the coldness of the bit comes into contact with the affected tooth, that the horse experiences the severity of the nerve pain. Nerve pain will not be seen by your horse dentist just by physical observation alone. This type of pain and the origins of it are often the refusal to accept the bit. Though of course there are numerous other causes for this also.

When the horse's pain pathway becomes damaged, this can lead to false pain signals being sent out.

Therefore there will be instances where physical injury has healed and yet the horse is still able to feel pain as if the injury were still there. Further to this when the horse has pain; the brain creates a pain map. The brain map sends out pain signals. Should the horse after a healed injury 'expect' to feel pain, these thoughts alone are enough to reinforce the pain brain map for that particular pain that can cause it to continue to send out pain signals. This is many cases is why diagnosis of pain and the location of it, can be so hard to determine. When there are no physically presenting symptoms, it is then likely that the brain itself is the issue. How do we fix the brain? It is not an easy task and on the outside of it, is veterinary medicine advanced enough to do so in all cases?

When nerves are removed or impaired (for instance in the case of de-nerving the hoof due to navicular) the nerves and nervous system will often seek to repair itself. When it this happens the individual may experience 'ghost signals' that will feel like creepy crawls walking over them. The nerves will try and seek out nerves that are similar to themselves to attach to and work with in order to rewire and repair themselves. This will also cause the brain pain map for the (for instance hoof) to associate with and overspill into the map of the area which it has now wanting to wire itself too. Due to this, in some cases, the horse may experience referred pain. In the case of Navicular it would not be wrong to suggest that even though the hoof has been de-nerved, that the horse may still be 'experiencing' pain in the hoof, due to the pain map in his brain still sending out pain signals. Being as the pain signals may indeed be constant. The horse's weight put on the hoof may have no baring on how that pain if felt or changes. This may give the outward appearance that the horse is now physically sound and pain free in his hoof.

The nerves as we have already discussed, in a bid to heal themselves, will try and rewire to those that are similar to themselves. The nerves for touch, temperature and pain are all very similar. Due to this these nerves are able to cross wire and create errors due to injury and including aggravated nerve endings. This makes an enormous amount of sense to me personally, as over the years I have come across several horses that for no obvious reason, have acted as if they are afraid to be touched when there has been no issue before. These horses have often described to me a sensation of 'prickly heat'. In these cases, for various reasons, the nerve endings were either damaged or being over stimulated. Due to the issues with the nerves they were rewiring and cross wiring to similar nerves in a bid to repair themselves. This meant for the horses involved, 'touch' was being experienced in varying different ways, or an abnormal collection of ways.

Heat

Itching

A prickling sensation

Cold

Burning

A tickling sensation

Electric shock type feelings

When a horse experiences an injury signals are sent via a pathway to the brain so that the horse knows there is a physical issue that needs attending to. Theory has it that along this pathway there are 'gates'. These gates are able to both open and close and due to this will have an effect on how the horse both perceives and experiences pain. When the gate is open pain signals will flow and may even be experienced as continuous. When the gate is closed it makes it hard for the pain signals to pass through and in many cases endorphins will be released. Now this sheds a whole new light on the varying thresholds of pain in horses does it not?

In my previous book Horsemanship - Myth Magic and Mayhem, I discussed vices and how they help the horse to release endorphins which are the bodies natural feel good chemicals and pain killers. Whilst the horse that is experiencing stress and anxiety may adopt a vice in order to release endorphins, the horse that is experiencing pain may also adopt a vice in order to release endorphins in a bid to relieve himself of pain. Some of you may also have heard of TENS. This is a simple electrical device that sends out signals that causes the body to naturally release endorphins and close pain gateways without the use of drugs. This is where it gets complex....

Some people may feel that the relief felt through the use of TENS is short lived due to the fact that once it is switched off and removed, those signals are no longer being sent out, the horse stops releasing those extra endorphins and the pain is back. Yes, to a certain degree that is correct, but let us look into this a bit further, as due to the complexity of the brain and nervous system, this without a doubt may not be the full story.

Not only is the brain the sender of pain signals and the creator of pain maps, it is also the one that creates pain perception. The horse's personality and mood will also govern how he perceives pain - both his thought and his brain are working in competition over how he feels.

Think of the brain as a computer. It can be programmed, deprogrammed, electrically trip and be restarted, spark out and be corrupted by things such as virus'. The mind, psyche, inner ghost (in our case the human that thinks and operates the computer) is the one that controls it, programmes it and in some cases tricks it. If the computer starts to fail due to a faulty programme we can do one of two things. We can either use thought and come up with ways to over come the situation that will fix the fault (in some cases this is possible but maybe not in all), or we can accept that it is unable to be repaired and the issue will continue. It is the horse's mind and thought that will govern when, if and 'how' that issue is dealt with and how it is fixed – if it is able to be fixed.

If nothing is done, chances are the brain - the computer - will keep running as it is (using the same brain map that sends out pain signals and reinforcing that pain brain map). However, should the horse choose to not accept that, think beyond the pain, not focus on the pain and not reinforce his pain brain map, he can in fact in many cases alter it and by consequence alter the pain signals that are being sent out. The opposite of this is also possible in as much as the more the horse focuses on his pain, the more he will perceive the experience of pain and create a reality for his computer that it is correct and that it needs to reinforce his pain signal brain map.

Once pain brain maps are created and reinforced, things can also go a step further due to the psychology of the horse. Once an injury has healed (for instance one that has caused lameness) the horse may have expectant pain. By expectant I mean that there is no physical cause for the pain, but that due to past experience, the horse may automatically expect it to be felt. If the horse's brain - his computer is by now not properly functioning, he may also now through mental expectation and brain map reinforcement, pre-empt the pain. This may cause his brain to send out pain signals *before* the physical action creates pain, or even in the absence of physical cause for pain, it may still be experienced even in the absence of a physical reason.

Now let us look at barefoot rehabilitation. Due to barefoot being such a vast subject it is not my intention to fully cover the subject of it in this chapter, but only to use barefoot transition as an example of pain and pain perception.

When a horse has metal shoes nailed to his feet he will lose to a large degree his ability for subtle expansion upon weigh baring. To better explain this I will use the muscle as an analogy. When a horse weight bares his muscle subtlety releases as it weight bares and then contracts as it is raised. The expansion allows for shock absorption and also stability when in contact with the ground. The shod horse in most if not all cases, due to the lack of this expansion will likely have reduced circulation in the hoof and lower leg and due to that most likely reduced sensation. As the horse has a small heart in relation to the size of his body, he also uses his hooves and the expansion and contraction of them to help him to pump and circulate blood through his extremities.

When the horse's shoes are removed, so long as the hoof is healthy and well trimmed, good circulation should come into play and with it, increased/ correct sensation. The horse is now better able to 'feel his feet'. This is where some horses will now experience a period of hoof rehabilitation for one of many different reasons, or experience no phase of rehabilitation at all. Often the act of shoeing and therefore reducing circulation and sensation will mask various different pre-existing pain issues.

These may include: Navicular and Laminitis which is why some Vets and Farriers will recommend shoeing for these issues. They do not correct the issue or reduce pain, they simply reduce the level at which the pain is felt, due to inhibiting the natural circulation and sensation of the hoof.

Once the shoes are removed and circulation and sensation is restored, the horse's feet will feel different to him. Let me explain this better. If we are barefoot and we run over stones or stand on hard ground, we will feel it and have the ability to adjust ourselves, our speed, how our feet land, impact etc in order to avoid injury (this is the barefoot horse). If we wear flip flops, although we still have the same level or circulation and sensation in our feet we can change 'how' we move as pain is not 'blocked' but we are cushioned from it (this is the horse that is wearing boots instead of metal shoes). If we wear shoes that inhibit our blood flow and our circulation and therefore our sensation, we will still be able to run over those stones as our sensation of pain is reduced. This is the same in the case of the 'shod horse'.

Once the newly barefoot horse is able to properly feel his feet, existing pain that was once masked due to inhibited sensation and blood flow may now be felt. If no pre-existing pain is present, he may feel totally comfortable on hard ground and yet be cautious over stony ground. Let us look at the various different causes of this.

The horse's innate friendly pain signals that tell him 'carry on doing this and you will injure yourself - you need to stop now'

'Ouch that hurts - I don't like the feel of that and it hurts me'

'Gosh that feels weird - I better move my foot'

'That hurt last time so it will this time - so I am safe guarding myself even though I do not feel any pain – better safe than sorry'

It hurt last time so the horse's pain brain map that has already been created and reinforced over time sends out pain signals before physical pain could be felt and creates the feeling and perception that it is hurting.

The physical anatomy of the hoof for various different reasons

Pathological forms of guarding to include muscles contracting to lift the leg, such as in cases of motor command and control

All of the above reasons are valid explanations for the cause of there being a rehabilitation transition period that some horses will go through after being de-shod. Though the why and how's of the experience for the individual horse will not always be easy to fathom. The point being is, if a horse is showing signs of rehabilitation, then that needs to be respected and he must be allowed to take his time with that in such a way that he can mentally and physically feel comfortable. For some horses it may just be a case of him needing to get used to his hooves that he now has a better ability to be able to feel what is going on and may or may not be helped with short term use of boots for riding. Whilst for others, the rehabilitation period and his symptoms may flag up serious physical issues within the hoof that need investigating and attending to.

Without a doubt pain and the nervous system of a horse is more complex than many of us will ever fully understand. I am by no means an authority on it; I am only starting to learn about the full extent of it myself. But the relevance and importance of it if only a little, needs to be understood by the equestrian world at large. As by the acknowledgement of what horses feel and experience, life for them, their welfare and how they are treated, can and will change. As will human minds once open hearts and compassion towards our horses' truly reins.

Some of our horses are in constant pain due to the environmental stimuli of light, touch and sound. Their faulty nervous systems interpreting these things as pain that radiates through their whole body. There is no such thing as a 'naughty' horse - not without cause. He may well be experiencing chronic, excruciating pain and with it confusion.

Pain for the horse can be his friend that prevents him from injury and pain can imprison him in a body long term from which he has no escape. We may not even know his plight, as maybe - just maybe - the pain is in his brain and not his physical body, but none the less is felt and experienced every waking moment.

Observe, listen to him, research and explore. Above all, never stop questioning the 'whys?'

NO BIT – NO BRAKES

The majority of riders will be riding their horse with a bitted bridle. Whilst this may be working well for them, it is also a good idea to get horses used to bitless bridles to see how well they can work. You could find that your horse works better this way and that they are more 'giving' due to the freedom they are then feeling through their jaw and mouth. A bit sits in the mouth on the gum between the teeth and over the tongue. Some horses will have a fat tongue that allows very little room inside their mouth for the bit to sit comfortably. The jaw bones have only a thin layer of skin and nerves sitting over them. Should pressure be applied to this delicate area, varying amounts of pain will be felt from the 'sore' to the sudden excruciating pain the likes of which we would be arrested for if we were to inflict it on another human being.

Horses that are ridden in bits will usually have had their wolf teeth removed in order to create a bigger space for the bit to sit on their gums between their teeth. If the wolf teeth are not removed the metal of the bit can knock, push and bang against the sensitive teeth. However, putting a bit in a horse's mouth is not an excuse for removing his teeth. When teeth are removed it is not only painful for the horse, we also risk them getting an infection in their jaw bone. For this very reason when starting a young horse, please do consider doing it bitless. If you find that this works well for you both, you can then choose to carry on riding this way and no teeth or mouth pain ever need be felt.

If you were to ask the average rider that rides their horse with a bit in their mouth why they do not use a bitless bridle for their horses, chances are you would get one of several different answers.

He needs a bit to stop him

He hasn't got any brakes unless he is wearing his bit

I would be too scared that he would run off with me

Hackamores are too severe

I am not allowed to use them in competition

He has always had a bit so why change it now?

He does not work correctly without his bit

He is happy in his bit

What is a bitless bridle?

Whilst all of these are reasons, none of them are particular valid so let's take a look at each one in turn.

He needs a bit to stop him

Why? Horses will usually run from pain. Should the horse have been treated and brought up in such a way that he has have developed the psychological state of learnt helplessness, where he just 'accepts' - he may choose not to run. However, this may not stop him from feeling that he wants to run from pain - he just mentally 'can't.

It may also be the case that he is an anxious personality with either a novice or a harsh rider. Whilst being ridden he may find himself existing in a heightened state of anxiety where he is neither able to fully listen, or concentrate - he feels the need to escape. The pain of the bit being pulled in his mouth in order to stop him may be so severe for him, that he has learnt that the moment he knows the reins are about to be pulled, he must stop in order to stop the pain or try and avoid it. If this is the case, you are stopping him through pain and fear. If you can not stop your horse without pulling on the reins and causing the action of the bit to come into play chances are your groundwork, partnership and trust are not in place.

Why would you want to ride a horse that you could not stop without causing him pain?

Why would you not be asking why he will not stop without his bit?
What is he actually running from, for or to?

He hasn't got any brakes unless he is wearing his bit

OK, so what is it about his bit that is causing him to stop when he is ignoring your other requests to do so? - Once again we come back to pain and the horse trying to relieve himself of pressure.

I would be too scared that he would run off with me

Why? Has he done it before? If not is this based purely on your lack of confidence due to you creating a false sense of security in the fact that he is wearing a bit? Why would he feel the need to run off if he was not wearing a bit? Surely he would prefer to stay with someone that he liked as he trusts their judgement and that they will keep him safe? Does this comment actually say more about you and your inner fears, than it does about your horse?

Hackamores are severe

Hackamores are only severe in the wrong hands due to their metal shanks that cause pressure on the nose and the poll when pressure is applied to the reins. When used gently and with respect and kindness they are not unkind. One of the other comments that I have heard people make about the hackamore is its lack of steering. We should not be steering a horse through his mouth head or face full stop! Direction comes from the rider and the aids offered by them whether they may be weight, seat or leg. A lot of people that comment that the hackamore is severe are the same people who have horses that wear a gag bit. Using the bottom ring on a gag bit is in many ways the same as using a hackamore, other than the horse has no bit in his mouth. It is all about what you do with your *hands*.

I am not allowed to use them in competition

So does this comment mean that if you were allowed to use a bitless bridle in competition you would? In this case we need to ask why the competition world is so far behind the times, and why it will not allow you to compete your horse in a bitless bridle? What are the organisers scared of exactly? Should you be going against your inner feeling and desire for your horse due to wanting to compete? Does that thought make your feel like you are compromising both you and your horse? If so then it maybe that the compromise actually is to walk away from competing in order to enable you to feel comfortable about what you are doing.

Some readers will have already seen amazing videos of competition riders competing in Dressage and Show Jumping. In some of these videos the horse and rider will clear their round or finish their test and then....the bridle is removed and they then repeat what they have already done without any bridle at all. So I raise the question again - Why will competition organisers not allow bitless bridles to be used?

He has always had a bit so why change it

We used to burn witches at the stake in the UK but we don't anymore - times change. Besides which, just because your horse has always had a bit it does not mean that he must always have one. Why not give bitless ago and see what improvements and changes can be made. If you never try you will never know how well it can work for you both. Experiment, learn and progress.

He doesn't work correctly without his bit

Then the question needs to be asked as to why he doesn't. What is it about the bit that is making him work as you want him to? And in fact, is he truly working as you want him to? Ideally he should have his hind quarters engaged and be working through his back correctly. If he is not 'on the bit' without a bit, chances are he is not using his body correctly as if he were, his head would automatically be correct and slightly in front of the vertical.

He is happy in his bit

How can you be sure? Horses are prey animals and masters at hiding pain. It could also be that our horse has become just resigned to 'it being his lot'. Just because a horse is not avoiding the bit, it does not automatically mean that he is happy with it so how can you be sure this is the case?

What is a bitless bridle?

As the title suggests, it is simply a bridle that does not have a bit attached to it. Like bitted bridles, there are many different kinds of bitless bridles all with their own 'action', each is designed to suit a different type of horse dependant on his ridden attitude, the level of your relationship and what he feels most comfortable with.

Nosebands

There are many different types of nosebands on the market and each of them have been designed to do something different. The cavesson when fitted correctly, is likely the only noseband that is not designed for a specific purpose other than the look of it and in how it finishes off the bridle. Now we will take a look at some of the other types of nosebands and what they are designed to do and suppress.

The Grackle

Designed to stop the horse from putting his tongue over the bit and crossing his jaw - rather than use a grackle, we need to be asking 'why is he putting his tongue over the bit and why is he trying to cross his jaw'. Once we have remedied the issues, we then have no use for a grackle and we have a more comfortable horse.

The Drop

The drop noseband is designed to stop the horse from opening his mouth. Unlike the flash, the drop noseband should only come into play if the horse tries to open his mouth.

The Flash

The flash is designed to stop horses from opening their mouths. If you are using a flash to prevent your horse from opening his mouth, please look for the cause of him needing to. My first horse came to me with a bridle with a flash noseband and an egg butt snaffle bit. She had a big tongue with a small mouth, the bit was far too thick for her and was designed to squeeze her tongue and hit the roof of her mouth. No wonder she tried to open her mouth! Her flash noseband was removed as was her bit and they were replaced with a side-pull bitless bridle. The only time I saw her open her mouth again whilst being ridden, was when we stopped so she could eat blackberries from out of the hedgerow.

Types of bits

There is such a vast array for the bits on the market that I feel that I do not need to cover all of them in this chapter, as it is likely many readers will be aware of them and likely to more of a degree than I am myself, being as I have not used them in many years. I will however cover a few bits of information that I feel are important.

The Snaffle

Many of you will be familiar with the single jointed snaffle. If you use one of these bits then please try the following exercise. Attach the reins to the rings of the bit. Put the bit around your lower arm and feel how the bit squeezes and pinches your arm when you ask someone to pull on the reins. This is exactly what it is doing to your horse's tongue. When you do this you will also notice that the middle single joint of the bit sticks out. This is the part of the bit that is hitting your horse in the roof of his very sensitive mouth and an obvious cause of him wanting to open his mouth – to avoid pain.

Most of us will have been taught that snaffles are mild bits, but as you can tell from the above exercise and explanation, this is not actually the case at all. The action of the double jointed bit will in many cases be lesser when used gently, but there is no getting away from the action of the single jointed snaffle which is often the bit of choice for children to ride in that have not yet learned full control and mastery over what their hands are doing. The same hands that are connected to the reins and the horses bit and his mouth....ouch!

The Happy Mouth

The happy mouth is made of plastic. In some ways this may be seen as more desirable as it does not have the heavy weight and coldness in winter of some metals. However, plastic is not as smooth and slippery as metal so in many cases these kinds of bits along with rubber ones which cause rubbing at the sides of the horses mouth can cause serious discomfort for the horse. As the plastic of the happy mouth bits is very hard, one simple chew on the bit can cause a serious sharp point to it that can all too easily cut, rub and hurt the horse's sensitive soft tissues of the mouth.

Whilst many readers may feel that due to the information that I have offered and the fact that I am pro bitless and do not use bits with my own horses may cause me to be biased. I do feel it is important for me to add that I have used bits in the past. I also have clients with horses that work well and are comfortable in their bits due to correct fit and light hands. Whatever we choose to use for our horse it is important that it is not over and above what it is that they (we) are needing. We need to make sure that the action of the bridle and / or bit is not just a way to mask a pain issue or lack of schooling. Just by our own feelings and actions alone we can unsettle our horse which causes him to become fretful. Just be sure that you are also not masking your own lack of ability or nervousness in a way that could be detrimental to your horse physically and cause you to 'bit him up'.

Now let us look at some of the things that our horse uses his mouth for that may be affected by his wearing a bit in such a way that his body is unable to correctly function.

His ability to lick and chew

He may produce saliva needed and created to digest his food and buffer stomach acid

His facial expression will be inhibited

His ability to vocalise will be inhibited

He may due to his noseband be unable to open his mouth to avoid pain

Distraction and fear due to pain, also causing a lack of focus

His ability to swallow may be inhibited, especially if salivating

He will be unable to avoid hands that are jabbing him in the mouth through the reins and causing him pain

Whether our horse is wearing a bitted bridle or a bitless bridle it is of utmost importance that what he is wearing is comfortable. Not only does he have a thin layer of skin with nerves sat just underneath in his mouth. This is also the case for his face. Should his bridle dig into his face, be too tight or sit directly over these nerves and press on them. Chances are your horse may well experience serious pain that he is unable to relieve until such a time the bridle is removed. When we put a bridle on our horse we need to watch his outward demeanour and his facial expression. If our horse is not 'closed down', chances are any concerns that he has over his bridle or bit will be demonstrated through his behaviour and expression, however subtle it maybe.

IS YOUR HORSE'S BIT AFFECTING THEIR HEARING?

Thanks to a wonderful horse named *Amber* and the information that she passed onto me, one of the first questions I will always ask a horse that 'spooks' when ridden is , is their hearing being affected when being ridden in a bit?

Since the communication with *Amber*, I have come across a large number of horses that are having their hearing compromised by wearing a bit. This can range from being very obviously affected to being affected so subtly, that the horse is not even aware until actually 'asked' about it. Out of curiosity I relayed this to both my Veterinary Surgeon and my EDT, both said 'yes' it is possible that the bit could indeed affect the nerve in the mouth that travels up to the horse's ear and potentially cause an issue with their hearing. Many of the horses that I have come across that have had this issue have since been ridden bitless and an obvious change in their behaviour has been seen. In cases where the bit has been reintroduced they have reverted back to the old behaviour.

Not only have I found that the bit can affect the hearing, but that it can also cause what horses describe as 'white noise'. By this they mean a low audible buzzing or humming sound, similar to what we would sometimes hear from electrical appliances. Although these noises might be very low and subtle, once a horse becomes aware of it, he tends to focus on it. By this focusing on it, it then becomes more obvious to him and can cause a huge amount of distraction and frustration to the horse.

Many horses wear bits all of their ridden life and cope well with them. Many have no issue with them so long as they are correctly fitted, comfortable and that the hands that hold the reins are 'soft'. However, even if all of these factors are in place, a horse can still be affected in the way that I have described above. So without a doubt it is an important factor to take into consideration when you are encountering behaviour when ridden that through observation and physical investigation shows no obvious cause.

There are many different types of bitless bridles all with different actions that if you haven't already, you may like to explore. One of my favourites is the 'Matrix', as this bridle converts to all of the different kinds. This means you will only have to purchase one bridle in order to see which type best suits your horse. This bridle is available from a company called Bitless and Barefoot (www.bitlessandbarefoot.com). Bitless and Barefoot not only sell many different types of bitless bridles, but also provide a hire service that enables you to try bridles with your horse before purchase, to enable you to choose which best suits them, before you make a definite decision.

It is an all too common to hear people say that they would not feel safe riding without a bit, as if somehow the bit gives them a false sense of security. The truth of the matter is you will not stop a horse in a bit if it truly does not want to stop! All you will do is cause pain and discomfort by trying to stop them by use of the bit and the effect it will have on the nerves and soft structures of the mouth. And as many of us know many horses will choose to run through and from pain and fear. If you cannot stop a horse through trust and request alone, would you actually want to sit on them in the first place? Physical intimidation and pain inflicted on the horses' soft tissues and nerves in the mouth is not a replacement for authentic respect.

Question, consider and explore

BITLESS BRIDLES

Now that we have dispelled with a few of the myths that surround bitless riding including that that we will fail to have brakes. We will now take a look at some of the options available and discuss why a bitless approach may be of benefit to both you and your horse when used correctly and with compassion.

The horse has numerous nerves and nerve branches, not just through his mouth, but also throughout his face. Not only can these nerves cause the horse immense pain when they are pressed, but they also need to be working correctly as they play a vital role in how the body performs. Some of the ways that these nerves function throughout the cranium and instruct the body are:

Eye movement

Licking, chewing and facial expression

Swallowing and the ability to control the muscles that operate the soft palate, pharynx and larynx

The horses sense of taste

Facial sensation

His balance

His sense of smell, vision and his hearing

His ability to vocalise and use his voice

Like any bridle and head collar the bitless bridle will sit over the nerves. For this reason as with any bridle, it is always important to pay full consideration to what our hands are doing. So long as the bridle is fitted correctly and is comfortable for the horse, it is what our hands are doing that will be the factor in whether or not the horse remains comfortable throughout his working life.

Due to the extensive nerves throughout the horse's face that are hard to avoid with regards to bridle design, any pulling and tension applied through the reins has the potential to cause pain in the same way that a bitted bridle will. Although the bitless bridle will of course be in contact with less nerves than the bitted one, as it does not venture inside of the horses mouth.

As with bits there are various designs of bitless bridle, each with their action and function. There is not solely one design or 'type' that will be happily accepted by all horses. For this reason it is always a good idea to start off with a bitless bridle that has the least action and offers the horse the most freedom. This is very much the same idea as bitting a horse down instead of up to so often find that 'less is more' when it comes to expected response and offering from our horse.

The following bridle descriptions are by no means comprehensive. There are many more bridle designs on the market, but here I will cover the most commonly used ones to give you an idea of how they work.

The Side-pull

Personally my favourite bitless bridle is the Side Pull. Its design is very similar to the head collar other than it has a throat lash. This means that if the slightest tension is applied it, it will feel little different if at all to our horse than a head collar, so it feels familiar to them. If we are able to suitably control our horse on the ground through correct groundwork having been put in place. Then it stands to reason that we should have no issue stopping our horse when ridden when that same level of trust and respect is present.

Side-Pull noseband
As you can see it has an extra pair of rings on the noseband - one at each side. This allows the reins to be attached in such as way that the end of the rein attachment does not cause any pressure to the horses' face.

The Hackamore

Next we will take a look at the hackamore. The hackamore traditionally has a metal shank at each side of it for the reins to be attached too. When tension is applied through the reins, the horse will experience pressure through his nose and his poll. Due to the length of these shanks, in the wrong hands the hackamore can be quite severe, but when used correctly it can be a valuable tool for riding. How your horse experiences the hackamore quite literally lies in your hands.

In recent years there have been new designs of the hackamore coming onto the market. This includes the Matrix that instead of long metal shanks has three rings, much the same as a gag bit. This allows the rider to attach the reins to different rings for varying degrees of pressure. The Zilco Flower Hackamore noseband is another option. As the name implies the sides of it are rings that are joined together that look similar to the petals of a round flower. The reins can be attached to various different rings that again like the Matrix, will cause various different levels of pressure. Both of these nosebands and bridles can be used on a setting where there is little if any pressure over and above a standard side-pull.

The Scawbrig

The Scawbrig, like the side-pull, is not that dissimilar to a head collar. Like the side-pull it has a throat lash and also additionally it has a moveable part on the underside of the noseband. Rather than the underside of the noseband being fixed at the side rings as it would be on a head collar. The strap that goes underneath the noseband, passes through and out of the rings on either side, where it then attaches to the reins. This means that when rein pressure is applied the horse will experience a tightening under his jaw as well as pressure on his nose.

The Cross Under

Although I am not strictly against the cross under bitless bridle I have to say that I am not fully convinced of it being a good design. A strap passes over the poll of the horse and crosses underneath his jaw, out through the rings at the side of his noseband and attaches to the reins. Many manufactures tell us that the action of the cross under is a 'whole hugging affect', - I have to say that I am not convinced of this. If we look at the design of this bridle it is clear to see that should pressure be applied to the reins then it is the poll that is likely to receive the most pressure. It is only by holding the reins out to the side and applying pressure to them, that the 'head hug' as described comes into play.

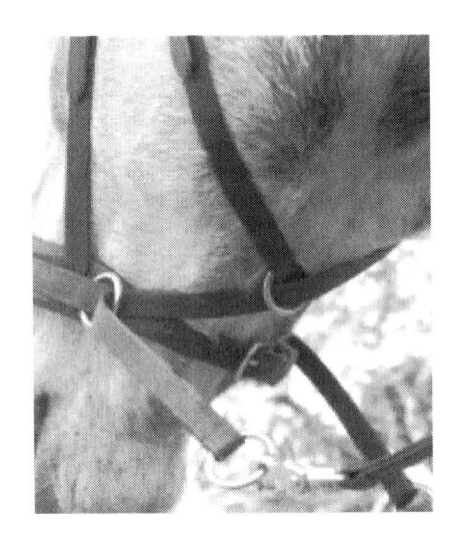

Due to the multiple pressures that this bridle is able to apply to the horse's head and face, it can be a little overwhelming for some horses. I have also witnessed quite a few horses that have head shook in this design of bridle. However, that aside, there are some horses that this bridle will work well for. As with all designs it is about finding one that best suits the individual that is expected to wear it. In an ideal world the rider will learn to work correctly from their seat, balance and legs, rather than using the reins for any form of braking or steering.

There are other designs of bitless bridles available. If you are new to bitless bridles, or are considering using one, a good place to start is the Matrix from Bitless and Barefoot. The Matrix is designed in such a way that it can be adapted to work in any of the above ways and may save you the expense of chopping and changing bridles in a bid to find one that works for you and your horse. Bitless and Barefoot also provide a hire service that enables you to 'try before you buy', to make sure that your horse is comfortable in the bridle and that it is working well for you both before you decide to make a purchase.

Whether you choose to use a bitted bridle or a bitless bridle, what is the most important thing is your awareness of your horse's comfort, his cranial nerves and how *any* bridle can be a painful and worrying experience for your horse when not fitted correctly. Also how we use our hands and our awareness of what they are doing, the softening of them and their quick release when needed, are foundational to both yours and your horse's ridden experience and enjoyment. The more comfortable your horse is, the more relaxed and responsive he will be to your aids and the happier you will be knowing that you are doing the right thing by him. Do not let fear have the overriding decision over the type of bridle you choose for your horse. Instead, put his groundwork respectfully in place and create a situation that enables you to make his bridling decision together - he will thank you for listening and for your consideration over of his needs.

THE FALSE GURU

Many well known trainers would appear to have gained a Guru status. Whilst it is often the case that we look up to those that we respect, it is not healthy to simply believe and go along with everything that they say and do without question. Those that have developed such a status for themselves have usually developed a system of training. These systems tend not to vary and adjust themselves to individual horse personality traits, or even take their personalities and histories into consideration. More often than not, there will be a fixed method for loading, starting, and all other areas of training. How a horse needs to be trained and how they best learn is very individual. For this reason alone, there is no one method suited to all horses. Most of the methods that these Gurus use are ones that will get results with little regard for the psychology and emotions of the horse whilst this training is taking place, nor the after effects. They simply use them because they know more often than not that they will bring the desired result and thereby make them look good to their fans - job done, sorted.

It must have been around ten years ago now that I wrote a short piece explaining why a certain trainer's trailer loading method did not stack up psychologically. Not only explaining why it was not in the best interests of the horse, but how it worked and why non the less. I put it on the trainer's forum expecting to meet with fire. There were one hundred and three replies to my post, ninety seven of which agreed with me and what I had explained. They were able to see not only why the method worked, but also how it worked, and why it could be considered both physically and mentally dangerous for horses. Strangely this is where it ended, not one of these people then asked for alternative ideas or offered anyone any. Nor after this time did I see any of them questioning any of his other methods.

I find this quite worrying as it shows only too well, how people fail to question the actions of their Guru. Even in this instance where they were able to see that this method could be both physically and mentally dangerous to a horse, they failed to question this or anything else about their agenda, intent and training methods any further. Whilst they were able to see all the flaws within this one area of their training, they were unable to fully accept it in a way that should ideally have caused them to question everything about this person's methods. This is a sure sign of Guru worship and it shows only too clearly how the Guru has 'captured' his audience in such a way that they are now not thinking for themselves. All they can see is the result he creates and the mental and physical suffering the horse experiences in order to get there, falls by the wayside. It is not 'seen' and it is not acknowledged.

He will have feigned enlightenment for his own glory and in order to bolster his own ego. He will lack genuine wisdom and even fail to see the genuine yet subtle complexity that is the inner horse. He quite simply created a tangled web of deception using his chosen method as he goes in harder and harder at the horse in order to create compliance. He will not release the mental and physical pressure from the horse until he has his desired outcome. To do so would make him seem weak to his followers. He may then have been seen to fail – he can't allow that. There is no way a charlatan will allow this to happen as he has an illusion to keep up, in order to make sure that others continue to bend to his will. Such is a psychological power and hold that the False Guru holds over his audience.

Most False Gurus are so in awe of themselves that they are likely unaware that they are not what they think they are. These people will be masters of deluding not only their followers, but also themselves by creating a live demonstration scene where this shared deception is created and enables him to captivate his audience - for all of the wrong reasons.

He will no doubt have his own vast selection of training mechanisms that he uses publicly each time he trains. Thereby creating the illusion that what he uses is much needed in order that his followers can achieve the same results that he does. No doubt it will be over priced and actually will not be needed by those that work over and above his own crude level. Those people that choose to work with the horse, listen to him and ask him to show them what he is needing from them and how best to train and instruct him.

Should any of his followers dare to raise their head above the parapet and question him in a way that he does not like, they will be spoken down to, ridiculed and made to look stupid - he will make a point of doing so, so that the next person dare not speak up. Such is his control freakism and his need to maintain the illusion that surrounds him. The False Guru can be dangerous, he is dangerous to himself due to his own deluded sense of self, he is dangerous for his followers due to his psychological hold over them and he is dangerous to the horses that enter his world.

Many of these False Gurus fly their flag under the umbrella of 'Natural Horsemanship'. By using the word 'natural' they are able to create the illusion that what they are doing to the horse is right, just and acceptable. There is nothing natural about what they do. Their act is staged, rehearsed and clockwork. They hand select the horses that they work with to make sure they will not be shown up by a horse that knows better than they do or one that is likely to question his crude methods. He needs a horse that will bend to his will and comply and perform as he applies 'his' methods in front of his audience as the crowd looks on in awe - how sickly. Of course if he is asked if he has hand picked the horses for his demonstrations he will deny it, or at the very least he will word his answer in such away as not to give the game away - his own version of his truth.

I have been to quite a few demonstrations over the years where these False Gurus masquerade. I have felt disgust at every one of them due to their rough handling and lack of compassion towards the horses that I have seen them work with. Some of them wear cowboy hats, ironic considering they maybe considered cowboys in every sense of the word. You only have to look at their facial expressions and their carefully chosen words to see just how well rehearsed and staged their 'show' is. Just as worrying are the facial expressions of their followers, sat mouth and eyes wide open almost spurting tears of joy. These people are failing to see the whites of the horse's eye, feel the tense atmosphere that is concerning him and the physical and mental pain he is enduring. They quite simply just see the false magic that the False Guru is by now a master at creating - never will he be a master of horses, it is just not within him and the horses know it.

You cannot con a horse; the moment one of these False Gurus presents himself to the horse, the horse knows he is dealing with a fake and a fraud. However sadly for the horse that does not spare him from having to experience forced compliance at the Guru's hands. It just means that the horse then feels more uncomfortable in the foreign environment of the school or round-pen that he finds himself. The discomfort creates fear within the horse, fear creates vulnerability and the Guru knows this - it is exactly what he desires – a need for the horse to seek a release of pressure – the horse surrenders.

He will likely have numerous minions; those that he has trained and allows to work under the banner of his name - for a price of course. The more merchandise they sell the more his pockets rattle and the bigger his illusion will become. They will be only too happy to work under the name of this 'amazing Guru', wow....how honoured they feel! Little are they aware that they are just part of his PR that helps to spread his name and method instead of their own. He will flatter their egos and make them feel special. In return they will defend him till the last. He will have already programmed them with all of the correct answers just in case they should be challenged. This may also allow his nonsense to extend to other countries so that his corruption spreads. 'Corruption' he shouts, 'No I am helping horses by communicating with them through their own language'....yeah right...

Sadly False Gurus will exist in all areas of horsemanship and horse care, not just training. They are found in the therapy and healing world too.

Follow your heart instead of the false illusion created by others to draw you in to their false pretence in a bid to feed their own ego. When you see these people work, rather than just observation alone you can use your body to also add additional information. In fact let us not use our eyes at all. Instead, we can just use our own body to give us the information that we are looking for by closing our eyes. We just need to think of the methods and reaction from the horse, including his facial expression when the training method is used with him.

Where do we feel it in our body?

Where do we sense it?

If we feel it in our head this means that we are trying to make logical sense of it.

If we are feeling it in our heart then this will mean that it is having an effect on our emotional state.

Is this a good feeling or a bad feeling?

If we feel it is our gut, how exactly does it feel?

Does our gut feel nervous?

Concerned?

Are we experiencing the butterfly sensation?

Or does it feel comfortable to us and come as an inner gut acknowledgement of truth?

Once we have completed this exercise we can then take it a step further. We just need to breathe, relax and close our eyes for a few moments. Now connect with the horse that we are thinking of. Imagine them in the training situation being asked to do something, as if it were us that were being asked. Breathe out again and sense where it is in your body that the information is being received.

Where are you experiencing the sensation in your body?

How does it feel?

Are you feeling nervous?

Excited?

Frustrated?

Does this feeling still resonate with the one that you had when you did this exercise as the horse person, rather than the horse?

Now step back and observe the horse as he moves in your minds eye. Look to his eye and his facial expression.

How does he look?

Is he relaxed?

Is he showing signs of stress?

Is he showing the whites of his eyes or a furrowed brow?

Are his movements soft and flowing or exaggerated, stiff and tense?

Our physical eyes are useful in observing the horse when he is being worked or he is at play. But what our eyes and our physical observations miss only too often, is how the horse *feels*. Being a prey animal some horses have the ability to hide their fears to a large degree to stop them appearing so vulnerable. Some horses will have also mastered the art of being able to mentally switch off in times of stress. This will enable them to not feel the fear in the same way that they usually would. This in turn will enable them to lower their heart rate and not display the wide eyes fear that so many do. Whilst this is healthy for them in as much as it stops their body releasing so many stress hormones, it also shows only too well the fear level the horse had started to feel that has caused him to have to adopt this survival coping mechanism in order to avoid emotional collapse. We need to ask ourselves...

What has led this horse to feel and master his ability to have to retreat into his survival coping mechanism in the first place?

As with so many stories there is also another side. In this instance it is that in some cases the false guru will be of use to some people and their horses. There are those that are unable to think outside of the box and are in need of instruction in the form of 'do this and you will get the outcome you seek'.

These individuals whether they are in equine or human form will have to a degree an inability to be able to think for themselves. They *need* and crave direction and to be told what to do and how to do it. They need the structure that the false guru provides— to them he is a saviour.

If this is their need then who are we to say they are wrong? If it works for them it works for them. It maybe that the horse involved no more asks the 'why's than the person that is instructing him does.

These people and horses may never see beyond him, may never question either him or his actions and the reasons for the outcomes. In doing so they enable him to continue – in the same way he offers them the same. Some would say in some instances the false guru has his place.

THE TRUE HORSEMAN

The True Horseman is the first that is able to put up his hand and say 'I think I could have done that better'. He is not afraid to admit this fact both to himself and his audience. Each and every horse that he works with he will adapt to and he will work in a way best suited to that individual. He will watch and truly observe the horse and may not do anything more than that for a while. His way is to first seek the inner horse. He needs to understand his likes, dislikes and his fears. He offers a hand of friendship to the horse that is not living in fear of this man who is listening to him. He knows his agenda and intent will not suddenly change and that he will not feel the need to flee from him – the horse relaxes in his presence.

The horse senses his low heart rate, the raising and lowering of his chest as he breathes and the lack of predatory eye contact from his soft eyes and facial expression. This is because this True Horseman is not asking anything of the horse at this time. Instead, he is enabling the horse to quietly observe him and assess him at the same time as he is doing the same with the horse. They need to get to know each other first.

The True Horseman will then offer the horse a neutral approach. By neutral approach I am meaning that it is neither positive, or negative. It is quite simply an offering in the form of a request that is open to different answers and the right one for this horse. Dependent on how the horse chooses to respond to that request will in turn, create the next request in a way that it needs to be offered. He will now know how the horse is asking for guidance and the form it needs to take in order to best suit this individual. Then the magic begins as the True Horseman uses his body, mind, thought and energy to communicate with the horse on a level that he is able to understand, feel comfortable with and respond too.

The True Horseman will lack ego. His concern is for the horse and he does not feel the need to impress his human audience. It is the response of the horse that he wishes you to see, he gives little thought to how wonderful you think he is. During his demonstration his focus will be with and on the horse with which he is working. Should his thought and focus stray too far from the horse, he knows that the magic of the connection will be lost at detriment to the horse. He does not want to create this anymore than he wishes to create a breakdown in trust for the horse, or concern for him.

The True Horseman also knows only too well that if his focus is too much towards his audience, not only is his focus not on the horse, but also that the focus of the audience will be on him and not the horse. This will cause their observation of the horse's responses to become lost. Unlike the False Guru he will not point out only the horse's responses that he wants you to see, in order to distract you from what he does not want your attention drawn to. Instead, he knows the importance of his audience viewing the horse's responses in their entirety, rather than a smaller distorted view that would 'prove' his method.

He will speak quietly to his audience, just enough that they can hear him. It is with this same quietness that he speaks to the horse with his voice, body and through his heart. He does not feel the need to scream out instructions or biased observations that he wants you to see. He knows the importance of clarity and wholeness for the horse, within his instruction and within the method being used - the method that has been 'chosen' by this horse.

The horse will likely be wearing a normal standard head collar, maybe not even that. The True Horseman does not need more than this as his intention is not to control or intimidate the horse. He is simply looking to seek a mutual ground with the horse that enables them to work together with co-operation. There is no need for restraint, pressure or pulling on his head and face to demand compliance.

The True Horseman will likely have come from one of two backgrounds. Either through a rude awakening to horses where he found himself amongst those that treated horses unkindly and got results through unkind means. He will have had the integrity to either speak up or walk away. He will have found his own enlightenment through following the guidance of the horses he loved and cared so much for. He will have known in his heart that the only true way to partnership was one that did not condone dominance and pain. Or he may have come from a background where the world of horses and horsemanship had only made itself known to him in his early adult years. He may have just gone in blindly and asked the horse to teach him what only the horse can. He may have questioned right from the start the difference between dominance and compassion and then chose his path wisely. He may have looked to certain methods, gone away, thought about them and returned to his horse with clarity and much knowledge of his horse and his needs.

This man is unable to dominate horses; it is not within his heart and psyche to do so. He knows that the way to the horse that creates mutual trust and understanding can only be gained when both he and horse are open, listening and willing to find compromise. He simply asks the horse to show him the way. He then catches up with the horse mentally and physically and they then once again can take the next step forwards together.

The True Horseman will not set an agenda for a certain outcome, he may have a goal in mind. But he will never force the horse in light of the goal. He knows that dragging the horse into his desired outcome in the long term will breed resentment, a loss of trust and maybe even a lack of confidence to the horse. He wants to keep the horse whole and integrated, not fragmenting his fragile psyche in order to feed his own ego and cause the horse just to surrender to his will.

The True Horseman does not feel the need to churn out unneeded merchandise, unneeded in the sense that it is unneeded by the horses with which he works. Nor does he feel the need to make you think that you need anything more in order to line his own pocket.

He is not setting out to show you and tell you what he can do. Instead, he is enabling both himself and the horses that he works with, how it can be when we work with compassion and openness and allow our ego to fall by the wayside. His love for the horse is genuine; it is not about what the horse can do for him, financially or otherwise. He quite simply just wants to help to make both their lives and our lives and relationships easier.

He will likely not be as well known of in the horse world as the False Guru. He will not feel the need to wave his banner and draw adoring fans to him. He knows deep down that those that seek true partnership and trust with their horse will seek him and others like him out. He does not mind whether it is him or someone else you find. He just hopes that the person that you do find is the right one for you and your horse.

The True Horseman knows that there is no need to argue with a horse. In fact he knows that should the horse argue, this is a form of information that he is offering.

I do not understand

I am not focused, please help me focus

I am feeling vulnerable and I need your guidance

I am physically and mentally unable to offer what you are asking of me

Please adapt your request in a way that I am able to best respond to it

The True Horseman will never tell you how it must be done; instead he will offer you a way forwards through guidance from both himself and the horse. He only asks that you consider it and not that his way is the only way. Instead he asks that you think for yourself and more importantly that you *feel* for yourself and that you find what it is that your horse needs from you. He then offers you his own his ideas and insights as to how this can be achieved. He does not tell you what to think; he asks you *to think*....and to *feel* the inner horse that you seek. He enables you to find your own path there; he walks beside you, not in front of you.

STATIC OBJECTS ON MOVING BACKS

For many years, the most popularly used type of saddle has been the type that has a fixed tree. Unless they have been purposely made to measure to fit the horse, no fixed tree saddle will ever perfectly fit. One of the issues with fixed tree saddles is that they are made symmetrically and no horse will be totally symmetrical. The horse will always have one shoulder bigger than the other, or some other kind of imperfection that will cause a symmetric saddle to never sit one hundred percent correctly all of the time.

Even in the case of a made to measure saddle the correct fitting may be short lived. The body of the horse is constantly in change due to various factors that include:

The amount of work and the type of work that the horse does

How the horse is fed

Health and injury

The changing seasons due to how this affects the body

The horse's back is never continuously the same shape as he moves. This will stop a fixed treed saddle from sitting correctly on him as he moves. Whilst it may sit correctly a lot of the time, it is logical that this will not sit correctly all of the time. Whilst the horse is in motion and the shape of his back changes as he moves, the fixed treed saddle will remain firmly in its shape.

Many years ago my first mare had the misfortune of going through a double colic surgery due to a tumour. It was six months later before I felt it acceptable to put a saddle onto her back again. My saddler came out to see her, looked at her back and stated 'They do not make saddles that shape!' Due to the surgery and physical stresses on her body, Kayleigh's body shape had changed, so the decision was made to have a made to measure saddle manufactured for her. Her new saddle fitted her well - for six weeks! Over that time her shape changed yet again due to her developing muscle as she was now back in work. I then purchased a second hand Reactor Panel saddle for her. This worked wonderfully. Each time Kayleigh changed shape the saddle was able to be adjusted to her. In just the space of five weeks her saddle had to be refitted three times. As this shows all too clearly, the rate at which the horse's back can change shape can be rapid. Just simply purchasing a saddle and using it for years and then wondering why your horse is bucking holds no logic. Saddles ideally should be checked three monthly - even more often in cases of recovery and when obvious changes are seen.

As the years have gone on new saddle designs have flooded the market that aim to try and fix these issues. Various treeless saddle designs, the Close Contact and the Reactor Panel to name but a few. These saddles aim to help the horse not only in feeling more comfortable, but they also adapt to the horse as his back moves, enabling him more freedom.

Those of you that have read my first book Horsemanship Myth Magic and Mayhem, will be familiar with my story about my past mare affectionately named Demolition Polly. Before Polly came to live with my herd, she had lived with a good friend of mine that was a Saddler. Polly had shown symptoms of head shaking in every saddle that had been tried on her. My friend had asked a Master Saddler to take a look, he had pointed out the ones that he felt fitted Polly correctly, but she continued to head shake. It was not until my friend bought an early edition Reactor Panel saddle from an auction purely out of interest - that Polly's head shaking stopped. The head shaking also did not occur if she was ridden bareback. In my friends words, ' I said Polly's saddle fitted her, the Master Saddler said Polly's saddle fitted her, but Polly said it didn't. In this instance after her previous sad history, someone was listening to Polly and was treating her and her opinions with respect. Polly never wore a traditional treed saddle again. When she came to live with me I bought her saddle from my friend to make sure that

Polly had the comfort and peace of mind that her saddle would not be uncomfortable.

I am not for one moment saying that treed saddles are bad for the horses back. I am simply raising a logical point for people to keep in mind when they consider the purchase of a saddle for their horse. All designs of saddles will have pros and cons to them. What is important is that whatever type of saddle you choose to purchase and use for your horse, it is the best one that you can find for them. Best does not always have to mean expensive. Horses are all individuals and some will have a preferred type. If we listen carefully to our horse and have his saddle correctly fitted and regularly checked, chances are we will have made the right choice. It is always worth shopping around and seeing what types of saddles are available that would suit both yourself and your horse. Whilst your horse needs to be comfortable, you need to be comfortable also. If your horse's saddle fits him, but does not fit you correctly, then chances are he will become distracted by your wriggling and lack of balance due to this. Before purchasing your saddle it is also worth looking at reviews in order to read about other people's experiences in order to help you choose correctly. It is also well worth exploring the idea of purchasing a second hand saddle that is in good condition. If the saddle is made of leather then this also carries a slightly more ethic tone, as it could be seen as recycling leather that is already in existence, rather than feeding the leather industry due to the purchase of new leather.

Many of your will have heard of the term 'bridging'. This is where the saddle does not fit on the back correctly and only comes into contact with the back in certain places. The saddle then creates a 'bridge' over certain other areas of the back. When a saddle bridges its weight is not distributed correctly and this can lead to pressure points. I will now give an analogy of how this can affect the horse's back.

Imagine a person stood on a trampoline. When the person is stood in the middle of it, it causes pressure in the form of a central pressure point. At the centre of the pressure point the woven fabric will dip where the weight is being applied. This will cause the fibres of the fabric to become closer to each other as they are forced together. This is the same thing that will happen to your horse's back. Pressure will be applied to the fibres of the soft tissues that make up his back. He will feel pain and over time damage will be caused. It is no good just padding him out with an extra thick numnah.

His saddle doesn't fit!

When a saddle does not fit your horse correctly and it creates pressure points. It will cause your horse to dip away from the discomfort. This in turn then forces the fibres and tissues of that area closer together as the muscles tense. This in turn will then reduce circulation and oxygen to that area. Over a period of time you will then end up with a horse with a sore back with tight muscles and who is in pain. When these muscles remain contracted they will pull on your horse's spine and may cause him to become wonky as he tries to compensate for the discomfort. The damage is done. Once this has happened, in time, the horse's muscles will create a new way of holding themselves. Once this has happened it will take at least twenty one days for those muscles to be able to go back to their original way of being – they will need help. They are unable to do this alone and the horse will need a body work specialise in order to help them. Three days after treatment, should the muscles then slip back to their newly found way of being, we will find ourselves back at day one. Your horse will need treating again and we are back to the twenty one day wait again.

Many of you will be familiar with the characteristic white hairs in small patches that some horses have on their backs due to ill fitting saddles. Their wither will most often be the place that these white patches of hairs are found, but not the only place. These are caused by long term pressure points that show only too well how much the horse has had to endure the pain and discomfort of an ill fitting saddle. Not only this but, it is also not uncommon to find nerve damage where these white hairs grow.

We now move away from saddles and instead turn our attention to the rider. Yes, it is not just saddles that can be static!

STATIC RIDERS

Many novice riders will feel nervous when they are sat on a horse, as well as those that are naturally nervous by nature, or have come into contact with a bucker or rearer, or have been injured in the past. When we are sat on a horse and we become fearful our body will tense. It will no longer feel fluid and be able to move with the horse in the natural way that it needs to in order for us to maintain our correct balance. We will likely be perched on top of the horse, rather than sat on him comfortably. This will be due to the tension in our body and our mind being distracted by unwanted negative thoughts. Our mind will not be focusing on how our body is feeling - only what our fears are in that moment and how we are experiencing them.

When we offer an 'aid' to our horse as a cue for our request, it will feel robotic and tense to him. This in turn along with our rigid body can cause him concern and not to be sure fully of what it is that we are asking of him. Whilst we may be offering our rather 'mechanical' cue, we will also be sending him out other cues that we may be unaware of.

The cues that the rider both consciously and unconsciously sends out to their horse, will often be conflicting in the information that it offers the horse.

The rider may be giving the horse the conscious cue to 'walk on', whilst their unconscious cues further offered by the body may be saying 'Please do not walk on, I am scared'. It will largely be dependent on the type of personality that the horse has, as well as his level of calmness and intellect, as to how he responds to this conflicting information. An anxious or an easily confused horse may experience an escalation of anxiety. This will make it harder for him to focus and decipher the information being given. This may in turn then lead to him showing his confusion in undesirable (but understandable) behaviour. It may cause him to run off, or it may cause him to refuse to move. It would not be unexpected for him to rear or buck as his way of showing his psychological blindness and confusion, due to his lack of understanding and fear.

The psychology of the horse's rear is either evasion, pain, or the inability to be able to 'see' that they can move forwards, or feel that they can move forwards - even when there are no physical obstacles in their way in order to prevent this. The psychology of the buck is due to pain or the horse's inability to be physically able, or psychologically able to move forwards or backwards. Thereby making him feel 'stuck' and rooted to the spot. At this time an inward energy will be created by horse that needs to be expressed in some way. The horse then makes a choice (that is often beyond his control) whether to emotionally and mentally close down in order to stifle the feeling of fear and confusion, or to expel the energy in the form of the buck or a rear.

Sadly due to rider fear, it is not unusual for the horse then to be punished for the outward expression of his emotional energy that he has felt the need to channel into 'behaviour'. At this point I would also like to raise these questions:

In situations as these, can in fact the buck or the rear honestly be viewed as negative behaviour?

Should we not instead see it as a form of information?

In situations such as these the rear or the buck is the horse's outward expression of the psychological impact that our request is having on him. The rear or the buck is simply his reply to our request. (I can't correctly answer your request to move forwards *and* backwards as you are asking me to - I am stuck). With this in mind how is he able to seek the correct answer that you are looking for, when two conflicting requests have been made together?

If the horse is naturally anxious or has been made anxious due to repeated conflicting request (which he may or may not be punished for), how is he expected to react?

What do you actually expect from him?

Do you think he is a mind reader that should know the correct answer?

Should he have to put up with these stressful requests at all?

Who actually got it wrong?!

Wallop - he is punished. He may be punished physically for his answer, but even if he isn't the stress it causes him to feel will undoubtedly feel like psychological punishment (whether meant or not), due to his kindness of allowing you on his back. If he moves away next time you try to mount consider if you have just added another possible cause for this to your list.

Now we will look at how we can help to correct this in such a way that it will become easier for both horse and rider long term. Sticking plasters are good for the short term, but your horse will likely be with you for years and it is of no use to either of you for this to continue and cause you both to lose confidence when it is so easy to remedy. We need to create long term change.

Breathing is, and will remain to be, the most important change that you can make for both you and your horse. When we slow down our breathing, our physical body changes as do the messages that our body sends out. Our muscles will relax and our heart rate will lower, our mind will clear and our tension that is being felt by our horse will disappear. We can further aid the relaxation by closing our eyes. When we close our eyes it causes us to focus on ourself and our horse, rather than what is going on in our environment.

The best way that we can achieve this without worrying is to sit on our horse that is wearing a head collar with a lead rope attached, and ask someone to hold them for us. This means that we do not need to worry about the horse walking off whilst our eyes are closed and that we do not feel the need to hold onto the reins to stop this from happening. This will also leave our hands free and not holding (clenching) the reins, further aiding in our ability to relax our arms and hands.

However, as we all know horsemanship starts on the ground! So we will roll back rather than run and before we even attempt to get onto our horse, we will stand beside him, breathe and relax our body whilst we quietly assess and work out all of the information that it is offering us. This may take a minute, it may take fifteen minutes. Once we feel that we are starting to relax, we can then open our eyes but we should continue with our breathing. Once we open our eyes it is important that we do not stare at our horse in his eye, nor should we aim our vision at his face as this is our predatory mode. Should our horse wander away from us during this time, that is perfectly acceptable and he should be allowed to do so. Should he choose to stay, then any releases that we feel him offer should be rewarded and acknowledged with a gentle scratch and rub on the wither (so long as he is comfortable with this). His releases may show in the form of:

Sighing

A deep breath out

Moving his back feet to rebalance himself as he releases his tension

Licking and chewing

A softening of the eyes and lips

Yawning

Lowering of the head

Each time you see or feel a release from your horse, after you have rewarded him, you will need to breathe out again as this will further aid him in his next release. Once we are feeling fully relaxed, our heart rate has slowed and we are seeing the releases from our horse, it is now time to .....wait for it....walk away!

This ground exercise should be carried out several times over a period of days. This will enable your horse to associate being in your company with the feeling of quiet calm. This means that when the time comes to mount him, he will already be in a much more relaxed state. This exercise must not be rushed; it is important that it is carried out in a time span that suits both you and your horse. The more relaxed you both are on the ground; the more relaxed you will both be when you sit of him. This will help lay the foundation correctly for the next part of the exercise and help set you both up for a successful outcome.

We are now ready to get onto our horse.

If we feel safe enough to, it is also a good idea to do this bareback, *but* you must feel safe doing this and so must your horse. Safety must be an important factor at all times.

Climbing onto our horse by using the stirrups to pull ourselves up will cause our horse to have to tense those very muscles that you have just helped him to relax. Not only this, but when we repeatedly keep mounting him in this way we cause him discomfort and can also cause his saddle to slip. If we ask the person helping us to give us a 'bunk up', then we can not stop the mount half way through should our horse show any signs that this is too invasive for him, or that it is happening too quickly - he needs time to prepare himself.

You already know what the next step of this exercise is, you will have already decided. But this does not mean that your horse does and he, like you, needs time to prepare!

For this reason it is important that we choose to use a mounting block or another solid object such as a fence that we can easily mount from. The reason why this is important is that if our horse shows any sign of feeling uncomfortable during the mounting process, he is able to move away so that he is not forced to stay which will cause concern for him. If he chooses to move away this is not him ignoring your request; it is an important sign that you have rushed him before he is ready to proceed. This just means that it is time for us to put our feet back on the floor and revisit the ground part of our exercise with him. I also feel it wise to mention that should he move away, it is also important to look to his physical comfort in the form of checking that his saddle fits and is comfortable for him. In order to rule out other issues that could be the cause of his moving away, rather than automatically assuming that the cause is due to how he feels, or how he is sensing we feel.

We now ask our horse to line up quietly beside the mounting block. We are *asking* him; we are not *telling* him. Once he is lined up quietly we can breathe out and step onto the mounting block and breathe out again. We now look at our horse in non predatory way and continue to focus on our breathing for thirty seconds. Should our horse choose to move away at this time, allow him to do so. Carry out any checks that you feel are needed, reassess your breathing and once again line him up quietly at the mounting block.

Once he is stood quietly (we are still focusing on our breathing at this point), we lift our leg and gently touch his back (if he is bareback) or his saddle, we breathe out and allow a couple a seconds to pass. During this time should we see him tense, depending how much he tenses, we will have the information as to whether we need to remove our leg from his back, or if we continue to hold it there to enable him to experience that it does not need to be concerning for him.

Once our horse is showing that he is able to maintain his relaxation with our leg in place and that he feels comfortable with it being there, it is now time to quietly and gently get onto his back. Once you are on his back he may choose to step forwards - allow him to do so. There may be some people that think I am wrong in saying that it is wrong to allow him to move forward when he has not been given the cue to do so and that part of his training is to stand quietly until asked to move forwards. I totally agree with that, but what we need to take into consideration is that at that moment he is feeling the *need* to move forwards as he is deep within though and he is learning to gauge how he is feeling. It is important that we do not distract him from this. As after we have repeated the exercise several times and we find that he has learnt to associate being mounted with relaxation. He will either not feel the need to walk forwards without being asked, or we can ask him to stand quietly now that the relaxation in him over the mounting process has become engrained and is consistent. At this point a relaxing, quiet mounting has become normal to him so it is not taking his focus away from himself and what he is experiencing for a few seconds to request that he stop, it is now not going to unsettle him if done correctly.

Our horse is now stood still and he is relaxed. The person helping us is stood beside side him and is ignoring him, in the sense that they are not doing anything that may gain his focus and remove that focus that he is directing at you and how he is feeling. The 'helper' needs to make them selves invisible to him.

We now need to bring our own breathing fully into our focus.

Each time we breathe out we allow our body to relax a little more. As our muscles relax our body will enable us to sit more deeply into the saddle or more deeply on our horses back, rather than us being perched on top of either. Our legs will feel heavy as they are now holding their own weight, rather than us holding their weight through tension in our pelvis.

We then start at our neck and feel for any tension. Once it is felt we take a deep breath in and as we breathe out we focus on the tension and we release it. We then work this way little by little through and down our body until we get to our feet. If we are finding it hard to release the tension in any areas, we can create more tension there by tensing the muscles, breathing out and releasing it. By creating the additional tension when we are finding it hard to release what is already there, it enables us to bring more focus to the tension, thereby making it easier to release it.

Once we feel that our whole body is in a state of relaxation we will also notice that our mind is no longer wandering to other things, or creating negative or otherwise unwanted thoughts. This will help us maintain our focus that is not only on ourselves, but we can now also maintain focus on our horse.

We can now give the cue to the person that is helping us, to ask our horse to 'walk on'. As he moves forwards we will now be aware that his body is also feeling more relaxed. As you have been doing this exercise, the breathing and releasing of your tension, your horse has been doing the same. This has also enabled his mind to calm and his focus to come back to both of you, rather than it being on his environment.

As your horse takes each step, keep your focus on his breathing. At the same time allow your focus to take note of how your horse feels beneath you and how his body changes with each step. Maintain your relaxation and breathing so that your body remains fluid. This will enable you to move *with* your horse, rather than his movements being independent of your own. You do not need to do this for long; even a minute is long enough the first time that you do it. Keep revisiting the whole of this exercise over the coming days *before* your ask anymore of either yourself, or your horse. We need this relaxing, focused feeling to stick and not become unravelled due to rushing both ourselves and our horse.

Whilst this exercise is so simple and in many ways will sound very basic, I can not stress the importance of it enough. This breathing and timing that we are working with, along with our newly gained focus is foundational to *everything* we do with our horse.

Practice makes perfect - or as near to perfect that works for you both!

RUGGING AND CLIPPING

It is standard practice in many countries including the UK, to regularly rug horses throughout the winter. We have all felt cold during the winter at times and the last thing we want is for our equine friends is to feel cold too, let alone get plastered in mud.

The truth is horses were never designed for rugs and rugs are poorly designed for horses.

A healthy horse has evolved in such a way that he is able to regulate his own body temperature. He will create and shed thick and thin coats according to the seasons and the level of extra help he needs. He may also have gotten into the habit of plastering his coat with mud in order to help him create further protection from the elements. The regular washing and shampooing of our domestic horses is not desirable due to the fact that it will wash away their skins natural oils that they excrete. These natural oils are designed to coat the hair and help make the coat waterproof to a certain degree as well as stopping the skin from dry out and becoming itchy.

Due to the horse growing a much thicker coat in winter (which for some people is visually undesirable), some people will purposely choose to rug their horses solely for the purpose of maintaining a thin winter coat due to the fact that they think it 'looks better'. Others will choose to rug their horse over winter in a bid to stop it getting 'dirty'. The regular rugging over winter may put a horse at risk of lice and bacterial infections if not regularly checked. This is due to the reduced airflow to the skin and the warmth produced that will enable bacteria to grow and multiply.

Rugging can further damage horses on an emotional level when left on for prolonged periods of time. Weird? Not really! As rugging will also greatly reduce the horse's ability to be able to engage properly in mutual grooming and also will have an effect on how we touch our horse and how that touch is felt by them. If they get an itch under their rug it is hard for the horse to scratch it, further frustrating them. Have you ever tried scratching an itch through a ski jacket? Not to mention the ridiculous practice of people putting duvets on their horse under their rugs, or multiple rugs on their horse to keep them warm as they have shaved much of their hair off in winter.

Have you ever seen a horse with a completely flat wither and back?

No?

Neither have I.

Yet the poor design of rugs means that they are designed for horses with flat backs and flat withers with no bumps in-between. I think to date I have seen only one advert for a rug that has taken the horses shape into consideration and made the design contoured over the back and wither. Little consideration for the horse and his shape is given when it comes to design. People want their horses to be warm in winter so they buy them, the tills rattle so why would manufactures go out of their way?

How often have we seen a horse wearing a rug that sits on his croup, sits on his wither and the middle of it is hollow until we push in down against the back? This will apply pressure to the croup and wither. It is just another symptom that shows us the poor design of horse rugs. Rugs that do not have integrated necks will sit just in front of the horse's wither and will often rub. I have seen no end of posts on social media sites where people ask how to stop rugs rubbing as their horse's are beginning to loose parts of their manes. The answer is simple - if you honestly feel your horse needs a rug find a rug that is designed properly and does not rub - not easy!

Due to poor rug design many horse's will suffer discomfort around their wither area when they are wearing a rug. Each time they put their head down to graze and they put their head up high, due to the fact that their wither is in the way....hang on! I thought rugs were designed to fit horses?! How can a wither be in a way of a correctly designed rug?

I have even seen one high withered horse whose rug lining had split due to the force and tension of it over his wither, due to him doing what he naturally had to do everyday - graze.

Imagine for a minute having to wear a shirt with a stiff collar everyday whilst you went about your daily business - one that came up to the top of your neck and rubbed the hair out.

Numerous adverts for rugs state that they are made from a breathable fabric. In truth most rugs unless they are cotton calico lined are totally made of man made fibres. The lining of rugs will usually be a 'slippery' man made fabric such as nylon or polyester in a bid to reduce rubbing. This is about as healthy for the skin as us wearing nylon knickers. A waterproofing solution is added to the outer layer to stop the rain getting in. Wait a minute? If water in unable to penetrate how can the fabric be breathable? Maybe many of the these manufacturers mean that the fabric was breathable *before* the water proofing solution on applied - oh that's ok then?

The idea of a rug is to keep a horse warm and dry. Yes other than the few areas sticking out and if it is waterproof and not leaking it will largely keep your horse dry. But once the wind picks up and lifts the rug (kept in place by the straps) cold air with get in and to a large degree he will loose his warmth.

Have you ever gotten too hot and taken your coat off?

Over rugged and uncomfortably rugged horses wish they could do this too. They are unable to until someone does it for them, so until that happens they will suffer and be uncomfortable.

The horse's body and its design is pretty complex, it has been designed for the job that it needs to do. Every single hair on your horse's body has its own muscle. When the weather is cold and dry the hairs will raise in order to trap warm air between them to help keep the horse warm. When we rug a horse it does not take long for these hair muscles to become lazy. This means that once the rug in removed the hair is no longer able to stand on end as needed to keep the horse warm. Well not straight away anyway, as it will take around ten days for the muscles to be able to adapt and get back to doing their job correctly.

There are many other things on the market to combat the poor design and fit of rugs. We can by extenders for wide chested horses, and we can by lycra and nylon 'bibs' that fit around the horses chest and shoulder to stop the rug from rubbing.

If your horse is getting rubs around his chest or his shoulders, it is because his rug does not fit him properly and it is uncomfortable for him.

Using one of these items may stop the rubbing to a degree and stop him getting sore patches and loosing hair, but it will not stop the discomfort of the pressure to that area and it will not make his rug fit.

Many rugs are still designed with leg straps rather than a fillet string (the string or strap that connects both ends of the rug and goes across the back legs behind the tail). Leg straps are dangerous. When a horse lies down he will often be sat down on one side with his legs pulled up closely to his body. When he gets up he will further pull his legs and feet underneath him. Each and every time he does this he is at risk of getting his feet caught in the leg straps. Have a feel of the skin of his inner thigh, there is very little hair there and it is a very sensitive part of his body. Leg straps will knock against this area as he walks. Ok he may get used it, but it is annoying none the less.

Let us also not forget that the horse creates his vitamin D from sunlight. If we rug our horse up to the nines we will lessen his ability to absorb the much needed sun rays. Over time this could have a negative affect on both his physical and his mental bodies. I will be discussing more about the importance of Vitamin D in a later chapter.

We now come to the other side of the rugging debate; the horses that may have ill health, low core temperate or difficultly in regulating their body temperature. There are many horses that due to ill health or old age find it hard to keep warm in winter. Just because a horse is not shivering, it does not mean that he is not cold. His core temperature is his inner temperature. His body may feel warm to the touch, whilst internally he feels cold.

We can liken this to when we have a virus such as the flu. No matter what we try we can not get warm and often the only thing that helps is a hot bath. Most of us will have experienced this at some point and will know how uncomfortable it feels. We know that not only do we feel cold, it also causes us to ache and for the older of us our muscles and joints hurt too - the horse is no different. Horses with arthritis that has taken hold or those with old injuries will also feel more uncomfortable. It may even be the case, that if the horse has had long term chronic pain causing his pain receptors to overly send out pain signals, cold may well be one of the stimuli that triggers or increases the level of pain signal that is sent out, due to the long term confusion of the nervous system and the brain.

This will in turn cause the horse's muscles to become tense due to pain, in turn the tension, lack of circulation in the muscles and lack of oxygen to them will create pain. Thus the ever eternal circle is created. Horses with a low core temperature may not feel internally warm being rugged, but in many cases it may go a long way to lessening additional cold factors that the body may interpret as a sign for the need to send out more pain signals. An ongoing cycle is created. This in mind, although rugging is far from ideal, there will be individual cases where it becomes the lesser of two evils.

Now we look at the clipped horse. The horse that has had some or most of his hair shaved off. There will be several reasons why people feel the need to do this, these may include:

Considering it more visually desirable

The horse sweats when worked

To make the horse look tidy in order to make it more desirable to potential purchasers in winter

Like nosebands, clipping styles also go through fashion stages 'the latest thing in the horse world'

The horse (such as in the case of Cushings Syndrome) may constantly sweat in summer. So in some instances it may be reasonable to just clip out a small bib to help relieve this whilst not over stepping the mark. It will be down to the individual case.

None of the above reasons other than sometimes the one is acceptable. When we shave off the horse's hair, we take away his natural ability to regulate his own temperature and keep him warm as needed for his health. It is all very well shaving off a horse's hair and rugging him. But once the wind start and his rugs lift, warm air is replaced with cold air. We create a situation where he is unable to help himself. Add to this his shaved tummy and other parts sticking out from under the rug and it is all too easy to see why it can cause such an issue to him. When the main of his body feels cold, he will pull the blood from his extremities further lessening the warmth in his legs. He is now cold and there is nothing he can do about it. His legs and belly are cold and the main of his body maybe over heating, due to numerous rugs and sometimes duvets. He can't win - he can't help himself.

Horses sweat when they get too hot; sweating is the body's natural way of cooling itself down. Once the sweat has dried the horse will be able to go back to his normal temperature. Of course whilst this process is happening, dependent on the environmental temperature, it is possible that the horse may feel slightly cold until such a time that he has dried. This is often the argument used as an excuse for clipping horses and shaving their hair off.

Now let us look at the other side of this and what happens with the clipped horse, aside from what I have already mentioned so far in this chapter.

The clipped horse has his hair shaved off. He is worked; he does not sweat so there is no (potential) cold cooling down period. He finishes his hours work, his rug is put on and he spends the next twenty three hours (possibly) over heating, whilst other parts of his body remain cold. Either that or, the wind lifts his rug, cold air replaces the warmth and he is cold all over. Try wearing a crop top in the wind and see how it feels.

Due to the way that so many horses are kept they are unable to find adequate shelter for themselves due to not having the full freedom to roam. It is of utmost importance that proper shelter is provided for them. By proper shelter I am not just referring to a decent hedge or a wide open shelter that the winds and rain can whip into, but proper shelter that the horse can go into through choice in order to remove himself from the biting elements.

My own horses have a system of paddocks set up. Other than one paddock that is the other side of my driveway, each paddock has a gate that opens up into the next. At the top there is an L shaped yard. At one end there is a big field shelter with rubber matting. At the other end there is a big open double stable that is not partitioned. No matter which paddock my horses are in when the rain and wind picks up they are able to go into their buildings. In their big open stables there are slow hay feeders. If the weather is bad for twenty four hours, they have no need to venture out into it unless they choose to do so. At no point do they need to stand out in the wind and rain unless they choose to.

Most horses cope well with cold weather and wind, they may not like it, but they cope with it. The issue for them is when the wind and rain come together. Often their thick winter coats may not be enough to help keep them warm. This is due to the rain flattening their winter coat and making it wet. Through flattening it their hair is unable to stand on end and trap warm air between it. Their by now wet coat is not keeping them warm and it is making them cold by the harsh winds and cold weather cooling the rain that is on their coat. A little like us dripping wet straight from the bath and standing outside on a windy cold day.

Horses need good shelter - they need to have an environment where they can make a choice as to how they chose to deal with the elements from one hour to the next. This will enable them to regulate their temperature.

After all of the above being said, am I against rugging? No most certainly not. As with many things to do with our horses some will have a place and be needed by our horse at certain times. I have had horses with acute illnesses, chronic illness and those that have a cold core temperature as well as other health issues where rugging has to a degree helped them either long, or short term. Would I rug a horse to keep him clean and so I could ride him? No I would not as other factors concerning his welfare and need for a rug need to be taken into consideration.

It is simply about applying good old logic to the situation that each horse as an individual is in. As well as weighing up the lesser of the two evils, the cold horse, or the risk of overheating the horse and affecting his ability to regulate his own temperature. This of course is aside from the healthy horse with his full winter coat intact, that may never have a potential need for a rug in his life - lucky him!

Over the years I have had numerous conversations with those that refuse to rug their horses even though they do not have adequate shelter for them. Some have told me that when they have seen their horse in the field during gales and heavy rain they are shivering. Some have told me that this is OK as the physical action of shivering helps to warm the body.

My message to those people is this: Try dressing your child in nothing but a faux fur onsie and get them to stand out in the field for days on end in the same weather - then see how quickly you have Social Services knocking on your door due to neglect.

****

Going Rug-Free

Over the past ten years we have gradually been changing everything in our horse's lifestyles that we felt went against their well-being. Of course what is in their best interests is not always obvious, especially when they have become dependent on certain things. We had been holding out against going rug-free for a long time, simply because it seemed like they needed their rugs, and we felt happier knowing that they were protected.

Finally we realised that continuing to use the rugs was a fear-based decision on our part for the following reasons: Anxiety about the weather, whether the horses would get ill or lose weight and whether it would cost much more to feed them. We worried that we wouldn't have time to groom them and that they might sweat when we worked them. We have been learning that the decisions based on faith and universal energy bring us closer to the truth, so we finally stopped rugging early in the spring one year, and we have never regretted it for an instant. In fact, now the sight of horses with rugs on is actually distressing for us.

At first the horses had to rehabilitate because they were dependent on their rugs. To a degree they needed the rugs because their own thermoregulation systems had been disrupted. This disruption was more profound than we at first realised. The most obvious aspects were that they were unable to adapt their hair positions to their environment i.e raise them when they were losing heat and lower them when they were overheating, and their skin couldn't regulate its oils and sweat glands properly because it was never exposed to sunshine or rain under the rugs. The majority of the horses went through a period of having greasiness and some scabs on their backs where the rugs had been. It was clear to us that this was a process of detoxifying and re-balancing, and by mid summer all of their coats were perfectly healthy. We didn't normally rug in the summer, but the rainy period in the spring was the first 'exposure' to inclement weather they had gone through without rugs, and that was what triggered the re-balancing in their skin.

That first winter we let them grow their coats undisturbed, and we noticed that the 'hotter' horses simply grew less coat. None of the horses lost any weight; in fact they seemed to put more on. They do have access to forage at all times, in winter they have hay in slow feeder nets all night and grazing in the day, so they are never without food. They didn't seem to eat more without rugs though. They were more active, playing and racing each other, and they definitely seemed so much more comfortable. Although we still had some residual worry about the bad weather, life was much easier for us too! No crazy dashes to get rugs on before it rained, or decisions about whether to take them off if the sun came out. It just seemed so crazy that we had been doing badly for years what horses can do so well.

They do have a 'horse-friendly' shelter which is a tunnel design, with a clear passageway through, but they use it far more often for the sun than the rain. One year they all got a chill from not having rugs on when it was too warm to put them on and then it rained and the temperature dropped. Now they can be out in cold wind and driving rain for whole nights and it doesn't bother them.

We were amazed at their resilience. As for working them, what we always want to do is respect what is best for them, so when we feel that their metabolism is slow and they need to conserve their energy for the weather, we rest them. When they are energetic and keen, we work them. Both of us enjoy it better this way. Not only that, but we have noticed that they don't sweat as much as they used to when they wore rugs and were clipped. To some it would not make sense, but in fact it is normal that they now have much higher tolerance for temperature change, and a more efficient management of their core temperature. Even on a winters day when the sun is quite hot here in the South of France, the 'teddy bears' hardly sweat after a serious session of schooling. Of course sweating is also caused by stress and nutritional imbalances and everything has to be addressed together. Our twenty or so horses are outside 24/7, they eat a low-sugar diet and they are all barefoot.

Since we went rug-free, we have rehabilitated several competition horses and observed the same lack of ability to regulate temperature in all of them when they were rugged, both in the heat and the cold. All of them have regained their cold-preserving abilities impressively, in fact more easily than their heat-lowering abilities. I will never put a rug on a horse again and I wish we had taken the plunge a long time ago.

Camille Dareau

Happy Horse Training

THE IMPORTANCE OF VITAMIN D

The horse absorbs vitamin D through his skin from sunlight as an essential part of his nutritional and biological needs. Horses that have black skin will be able to absorb the sunlight to a lesser degree than those that have a lighter coloured skin. There are pros and cons to the colour pigmentation of skin. Whilst the black skinned horse may have a harder job in absorbing enough of the sun's rays, the pink skinned horse will in some cases be more prone to other issues such as sunburn, skin photosensitivity and mudfever.

Due to the way in which so many horses are kept and the common practice of stabling horses and rugging them, many are not exposed to the suns rays and able to absorb them as much as they need to. Due to the fact that their routine is usually kept the same, there is little chance of a horse that is suffering from deficiency being able to correct this without changes being made.

Vitamins D2 and D3 are needed by the horse in order to correctly absorb, transport and deposit both calcium and phosphorus throughout their body. Studies have shown that if a horse is lacking in Vitamin D, then chances are he will have an issue with the level of calcium absorption that he is able to have from his food alone. This can cause the body to 'pull' calcium from the bones in such a way that in the long term the integrity of the bone may become compromised due to the fact that vitamin D is manufactured by the body through the sun's rays. Many commercial horse feeds on the market today have low levels of vitamin D in them which may not be enough to make up for the horse's natural deficiency - he is in a situation where he can't win and he can't help himself.

The ways in which a horse's health can be affected by a deficiency in Vitamin D are numerous. A long term deficiency can lead to issues such as:

Swollen joints

Weak bones and teeth

Lameness

Certain cancers (most commonly Melanomas)

A lesser resistance to stress through work and environmental factors

Issues with 'tying up' and muscle cramping

A weakened immune system

A greater risk of laminitis due to the links between insulin resistance and laminitis

Vitamin D2 and D3 are needed by various different receptors in the organs of the horse's body. Most if not all of the D3 will come by way of the self manufacturing process that the body goes through due to the sun ray absorption. Many horses however will need supplementation of vitamin D in their food.

Not only does Vitamin D play a vital role in the correct functioning and health of the horse's body, but it also plays a role in their mental wellbeing also.

If a horse is deficient in Vitamin D this will also leave him wide open to developing Equine Seasonal Affective Disorder (ESAD - also known as 'the winter blues'). Whilst it is perfectly understandable that the cold and wet weather climates of many countries and the fact we have less daylight hours during the winter can be depressing in itself. An insufficient supply and absorption of vitamin D during this time can also cause depression in many of our equine companions.

Many of the symptoms of depression in our horses are similar to those of pain and so for some horse owners, trying to work out how their horse is feeling and if the issue is physical or mental in nature, can be difficult.

Some of the possible symptoms of Equine Seasonal Affective Disorder are:

The horse interacting less with others, or standing alone

A lack of interest in their work

A lack of interest in their food

Lack of their normal personality and increased 'quietness'

Lack of tolerance towards being touched

'Grumpy' face

Sadly many in the Veterinary profession do not place as much importance on vitamin D as it so rightly deserves. If you think that your horse maybe deficient in it, it is well worth looking into to see how the imbalance may be addressed through how you both manage your horse and his diet.

MUDFEVER AND SCRATCHES

Many of us at some point will have either known a horse, or presently have a horse that is prone to mudfever. The titles 'Mudfever and Scratches' are somewhat misleading for this medical issue. Mudfever is not caused by mud, anymore than it is caused by scratches. The mud and moisture simply provide an ideal environment for the mudfever to take hold due to other issues going on with the body. For this reason it is not at all unusual for a herd of horses to be turned out in a muddy field in winter with only one of two of them having an issue with it.

There has to be a precursor

In most cases this precursor will be lowered immunity through a lack of correct nutrition. This can be further escalated as if the correct nutrition is not in place, the barrier between the sodium and potassium of the skin cells will be weak, leading to 'leaky cell syndrome'. This means that the skin itself will be weak which then allows the bacteria to have a detrimental affect on the skin in such a way that mudfever is able to occur.

There are no end of topical applications on the market to put on mudfever and also to help provide a waterproof barrier on the skin to help to keep it dry. Whilst in some instances this can be useful as many of these applications will have healing ingredients in them, some can also be harmful. I have often heard people give the advice that pig oil is good for creating a waterproof barrier for mudfever. Pig oil does not come from pigs; pig oil is a mineral oil. Often when people hear the word 'mineral', they often assume that mineral is good. Mineral oil is not good; is made from crude oil which is cancer causing and along with some other topical applications, it will suffocate the area of skin that it is applied to.

Often when the horse's legs are dry the scabs will crack, further creating the potential for infection to set in. The cracks will be sore and will be slow to heal. For this reason some topical applications can be useful. Personally my favourite is cold pressed neem oil. This is anti bacterial, anti inflammatory and it is easy to apply. I purchase mine from a company called bitless and barefoot. So that's the outside of the horse sorted - now let's look at the inside.

In earlier paragraphs I mentioned 'leaky cell syndrome' and how this can play a role in the onset of mudfever by allowing the bacteria to take hold. So how do we help to make these leaky cells healthy again? This is done through the use of remedial nutrition. Remedial nutrition basically means nutrition (usually additional to the existing) that the horse is given for a period of time and not indefinitely as a way of helping the body to heal and kick start it into doing just that.

My favourite remedial product for doing this is a product called TPGS5 from www.trinity-consultants.com. TPGS5 contains high doses of water soluble vitamin E, potassium and lots of other lovely goods that are needed by the body in cases of cellular repair. It is mixed into a honey base and the horse only need be fed one teaspoon of it twice a day in order to see dramatic healing occur in a short space of time. In the past there have been times when I have seen this product used alone heal mudfever in the middle of winter whilst the horse lives out in a field with no topical applications applied to the mudfever areas.

The bacteria that is most often present with mudfever is Dermatophilus and sometimes also Staphylococcus. Mudfever can also be caused by dermatophytes (fungal organisms), which is why sometimes mudfever can been seen in the spring and autumn when no mud is present, due to damp heat that is a perfect breeding ground for it. These same fungal organisms and bacterias also cause 'rain scald' - 'rain rot' on other areas of the body, such as under the stomach where mud has splashed or the horse has lied down a lot on damp, wet ground.

There are several other reasons that a horse may also get mudfever. These will include: Chorioptic mange mites and photosensitivity. Mudfever can appear on just one of the horse's legs, or it may be on all of them. Chances are if your horse has a white leg with pink skin, the mud fever will likely appear there first, due to the lack of pigmentation in the skin.

When mudfever appears many owners that are used to seeing it each winter will slap a bit of cream on it and either turn the horse out, or stable him with little thought. I can not stress the importance of taking mudfever seriously enough. In some cases when not treated properly and allowed to get worse, serious infection can take hold and the horse can die. Often with mudfever, vascullitis (inflammation of the blood vessels) will occur and should a Staphylococcus infection suddenly get out of control, your horse is in trouble! I have seen an infection take hold so quickly that the horse almost died. Within two hours the horse that was already on antibiotics went from a low grade infection to one that could have killed him in hours. It took forty minutes for the vet to arrive and the horse trailer was hooked up ready to take him to hospital. During the forty minute wait, the hair started to fall out of his skin in clumps, his leg swelled and he was in obvious pain. Luckily for this horse intravenous antibiotics worked within minutes and so a mad dash to the local hospital was avoided. It took him a full three months to fully recover physically. Had he not have been checked that night he would have been dead by morning. Such was rapidness and ferociousness of the infection.

Repeated bad cases of mudfever in the same area will also risk weakening the skin and could cause scar tissue. Scar tissue is far more vulnerable to injury and infection than healthy skin. Bad cases of mudfever can also lead to permanent hair loss and proud flesh - like I said - do not take mudfever lightly!

THE EQUINE OLFACTORY SYSTEM

The horse's olfactory system is used by him for olfaction, in other words for his sense of smell. His primary olfactory system is used for detecting volatile and airborne substances, whilst the secondary part of his olfactory system is used to sense fluid phased stimuli. The horse's olfactory system is extremely sensitive, even to the point that it enables him to sniff the droppings of a fellow herd member and be able to determine whose droppings they are. He also uses his olfactory system to gain information about others through his ability to smell pheromones.

The olfactory system goes one step further in as much as it also enables the horse to decipher the different scents around him and take those into his perception. This is an invaluable tool for him, as it enables him to gain information about the health and emotional state of others, as well as enabling him to sniff and seek out his own medication and nutrition that may be growing wild in his environment.

When we choose to use chemical based substances on our body, as well as for washing our clothes in them, we can confuse our horse's olfactory system and cause him to have to search within the different scents for the correct information that he is seeks.

Being as our horse's olfactory system is far more sensitive than our own, what may smell nice to us and be mild, can literally over power his own sense of smell and cause him to want to move away from it. Our expensive perfumes, washing powers and other chemical scents we choose to wear are neither desirable or helpful to him. He prefers you to smell like you!

As the years have gone on, we have started to keep our horses in smaller paddocks and have created more physical boundaries for them and in doing so we have removed their ability to roam in a way they were once able to do with more freedom. Add to that our use of pesticides and herbicides and we are to a large degree destroying our horses' natural environment. Many of the sprays that are used today kill weeds; weeds to us, but in so many cases medicine and nutrition for our horses.

Whilst weeds such as ragwort are highly toxic to our horses, many will also have a positive medicinal effect when needed and self selected by the horse. Wintergreen for instance is highly toxic to marine life and yet for some horses it can be a powerful and fast working pain killer.

The practice of horses self selecting their own medication and consuming medicinal herbs and other plant matter is called Zoopharmacognosy (Equine Aromatics). I am pleased to say that it is fast becoming understood in the mainstream equestrian world and is now widely used by professionals and horse owners alike that are seeking to help their horses' regain their natural health.

The aromatics may be offered in several different forms which may include:

Essential oils

Mascerated oils (base oils that have had herbs in them for several weeks and are then filtered)

Plant based powers

Fresh and dried herbs

Chalks and clays

When these plant and naturally occurring substances are 'offered' to the horse, he will sniff them and use his olfactory system as a way of gaining information about them. No matter how a plant may smell and whether it is bitter or it has an undesirable sensation such as stinging, the horse will choose to select it regardless if the information that is received by way of his olfactory system is telling him it will be of benefit to his health. When a horse is in desperate need it is not unusual for him to scream for and grab at the aromatics. Although this is often done politely the desperation at times can be clearly seen none the less.

The reason that the horse must be allowed to self select his own medications is that each substance will be very specific to his needs. It maybe that he has an infection and that five or six oils that have anti-bacterial properties are offered to him, but it maybe that only one of the oils contains the exact medicinal properties that only he knows that he needs and in what quantity.

Around five years ago I went out to my field to find on of my horses on three legs and hopping lame. His hoof was very warm to the touch and he was very quiet and unhappy. I went with my gut feeling to give the aromatics a try before I called his vet. If I did not see any signs of improvement within a few hours, then I knew it would be essential to call out his vet in order to administer him with pain relief and antibiotics to deal with the presenting symptoms.

I luckily had quite a few different essential oils and other concentrated plant materials available, so I tried offering each of them to him in turn. I had offered him around four different substances with no interest or reaction from him whatsoever. Next I offered him seaweed absolute which has antibacterial properties as well as nutritional ones. His reaction was instant. He sniffed the bottle and waved his front leg in the air as I was not able to get it out of the bottle fast enough for him. In a space of two minutes he licked his way through ten mils. Essential oils, absolutes (and in some cases extracts) are so concentrated that many of them when sniffed or licked by the horse are able to be detected in the blood stream within minutes. Only three hours later, not only was the heat from his hoof gone, but he was fully sound to the point of cantering around his field and playing with his friends. However this was not the end of the issue.

Once my horse had licked his way to the bottom of the bottle he was still showing an interest in it. His interest was displayed as his need to rub his face on my hands. Every time I tried to walk away, he would stand in front of me sideways and shift himself should I try and move again. No matter which direction I tried to walk away in he would position himself to prevent me leaving. Sadly I was unable to offer him what was no longer in my hands.

Within six hours my horse's symptoms returned and once more his hoof was very hot and he was lame. By then I had been able to source more of the seaweed absolute for him, this time thirty mils, which he managed to lick his way through within ten minutes. He then only began to lose interest as he started to reach the last few drops in the bottle. The same result was observed as had been earlier in the day. Three hours and again the heat was gone from his hoof and he was sound and no longer lame. This time I am pleased to say that his symptoms stayed at bay and his soundness remained. However, this was only the beginning of a very interesting observation of not only him, but also my other horses and how through my observations of them and their needs, other horses were able to be helped too. The next few days I spent observing my horses and their reactions and intake of seaweed was to largely change my understanding of seaweed and its medicinal properties as well as its nutritional ones.

SEAWEED

The days that were to follow the healing of Alfi's lameness were certainly to prove to be interesting ones. After he had returned to soundness, there was no further request or reaction from Alfi towards seaweed for the rest of that day. However, the next morning he was taking an obvious interest in the seaweed that was on my jacket due to me wiping my hands on it the day before. I was unable to source more seaweed that day for Alfi, other than in its granulated form.

I emptied a mug of seaweed into a food bucket, added water and offered it to him. His reaction was instant. He instantly started to drink from the bucket, followed by him purposely collapsing to his knees in order to try and get his head into the bucket in a bid to splash as much of the seaweed water over his face as he was able too. Each time Alfi emptied a bucket, I refilled it and so this went on as he continued to drink and grasp at the now soft granules that sunk to the bottom of the bucket. Six kilos of dry weight seaweed later he lost interest, that was it for day one.

The following day Alfi's interest had returned. This time he consumed around three kilos of soaked seaweed. Whilst less than the previous day, this was still a massive quantity compared with what the information is that is printed on numerous feed sacks, what we are told to use by our veterinary surgeons and what is advised by numerous articles on the internet. All of which would largely have warned again such quantities and even warned of arsenic and other heavy metal poisoning.

I have to admit at this point I was starting to feel pretty apprehensive. By rights, by offering Alfi these kinds of quantities I was going against everything that I had read to date. However, had I fully trusted everything I had read to date and allowed fear to get in the way, I would have never seen the results that were about to manifest.

Altogether Alfi's seaweed intake continued daily for around a week until it showed any indication of declining and then only slightly for a total of four weeks. During this period of time I saw no change in his outward demeanor, droppings or health in general.

One of the health issues that had remained an enigma with Alfi for years was his grossly swollen sheath and at times his lower hind legs. Despite having been examined by three different veterinary surgeons the most feedback and explanation I was able to get was, 'lots of geldings have swollen sheaths (so that makes it normal then?) to 'I don't know' and 'lots of horses get filled legs'. None of these answers were welcomed or satisfactory, they were simply an excuse and vocalisation of 'I do not know and you are asking me something out of my field even though it is a common story - full stop'. In other words I had wasted my money and the vets involved did not have a clue how to resolve the issue or the true cause of it - not helpful! No wonder I had to put my faith into Alfi's 'hands' and trust his instincts and innate knowing in the absence of those that should have been able to provide the answers for me to help my horse. Those that had been trained in nutrition, biology and physiology as well as biochemistry - it paid off.

Typically it was not until later that I spoke to a vet whose wife had opted out of allopathic medicine and into herbal medicine, as well as someone who worked with remedial nutrition, that both gave me the same answer. 'He was balancing his electrolytes'.

That was quite a few years ago now. Being as Alfi's 'seaweed' bucket was left out on the yard to allow him to self select as needed, it was not long until I saw my other equines doing the same. Since this time I have offered my horses many different forms of 'salt'. This has ranged from the commercial salt licks that are available easily through out agricultural stores, to Himalayan salt, sea and rock salt. No matter what form it is offered my horse's choice is always the same - seaweed. All other forms have been ignored.

It stands to reason that if my horses are choosing to self select seaweed in varying quantities that this will change according to the seasons, their sweating in warm weather and their 'lesser' needs in winter. To a certain degree this is true, but I have also seen definite patterns of intake that I have found does not follow the pattern of the seasons. So the only thing I can put this down to is, the innate needs of the body of the individual from day to day, for which I have now given up trying to rationalise.

In light of the science and nutritional advice available, over and above my own knowledge, it is not for me to tell anyone that they should go against knowledgeable information when it comes to their horse's health. All I can offer through years of daily observation and result is the facts that I have witnessed and how I have seen my horse's health improve when much of the information that I have read goes against reason and my horse's choices.

What has also interested me is the results seen by others, who through their own choice have also chosen to try the 'seaweed approach'. Again, like myself, these are people that were having poor results following advice for laminitis, filled legs, swollen sheaths and teats - people that have gone in search of their own answers and looked to their horses to provide those answers. The results? I have yet to hear of a horse or pony that has not improved. I have also yet to hear of a horse or pony that through their intake of seaweed has gotten arsenic or copper poisoning as scare mongering articles would have us believe will happen.

I am not by any means suggesting all horses should be put on a diet of ad lib seaweed, neither am I suggesting that seaweed is the be all and end all answer to all equine illnesses. What I am suggesting is that seaweed, a nutritional, antibacterial electrolyte rich food that nature provides, should without a doubt be further researched with an open mind and the existing results taken into consideration.

Whether we choose of offer our horses seaweed on an ad lib basis, or put the often recommended twenty to thirty grams into their food a day, chances are we are helping our horses in their nutritional needs.

So what does seaweed contain and why is it so nutritious? Seaweed contains on average fifty six different vitamins, minerals and trace elements. The exact amounts of each will be largely dependent on the area harvested. It is also incredibly important that any seaweed has been tested in order to check that its natural balance of minerals or heavy metals is not abnormal. Equally as important is that the seaweed that we feed our horses has been harvested from a clean and trusted source that has been correctly and well filtered so as to remove sand that could potentially cause colic in our horses.

Should you suspect that your horse may have sand in their gut from previous feeding, sandy soil or from turning out in a sand school, an easy test to do is to get a few balls of their poo and put it in a bucket of cold water and let it dissolve. If sand is present it will float to the top of the water. You can then look into feeding psyillium husks or something similar to help pick up the sand from the gut and remove it through their droppings.

The following is just a short list of what can be found in seaweed and is in no means comprehensive.

Calcium - Needed for skeletal health, heart health and the horse's nervous system function

Magnesium - Helps to activate enzymatic activity and is essential for heart health

Potassium - Naturally aids in the prevention of high blood pressure and help to provide cellular energy)

Sodium - Essential for the correct balance of body fluids - often considered to be our internal 'ocean')

Iron - As hemoglobin, it transports and aids in the distribution of oxygen to all of the horses' cells)

Iodine - Plays a huge role in thyroid health

Chromium - Works with insulin to help to regulate blood sugar

Copper - Helps to protect the nerve sheaths, also helps to build supple arteries and is required for iron absorption

Absorbs and eliminates (at the least reduces) radioactive elements and heavy metal contaminants from horses' bodies.

STABLING VS FREEDOM OF MOVEMENT

For many years the stabling versus freedom of living out debate has continued. In an ideal world our domesticated horses would, along with nature, dictate a firm answer. The mental state of our domesticated horse's and how they have been forced to live and the mental consequences of that, along side the practical realities of where we keep them, have created a situation where the considerations and answer is no longer easy, available or a hard and fast rule.

In an ideal world there are many factors to take into consideration and also boundaries with which we to a degree are bound to.

Many horse owners are in the situation where they do not own their own land and therefore, livery stables are their only option. Let us not forget that the 'average' livery yard is a 'business'. The more horses they can fit in and the more they can supply for yours and your horse's personal needs, the more they can charge and the better their profit will be.

Due to this in the UK, the most common livery option is stable (the price goes up) with limited turnout - or on a better note, full turn out during the drier months, or maybe if you are lucky all year round. Immediately a stable commands more rent for the yard owner and the owner then cops the further costs in the form of bedding for their horse if the yard owner supplies it to their clients. This enables the stable yard to have to worry less about the turnout acreage offered, the level of grazing and in some instances will also save them further costs in land management in the form of harrow, rolling and reseeding. Whilst the owner mucks out and pays for the privilege of a roof (often a leaking one) over their horse's head, often (solitary confinement) and a dry horse.

When put in those terms it kind of brings things into perspective does it not?

This of course is not how all livery yard owners conduct themselves - for some the supplying of livery is carried on a vocational level, rather than purely a business one.

Once that stable door is closed, that is your horse's home until such a time as you return or someone else does and releases the bolt that keeps him there. He is dry, he has hay (we hope), if he is lucky he has his friend next door and your livery yard owner has their rent - job done sorted.

This is the way in which many horses and their owners have entered into the horse/ownership world and for many it is the 'norm', it is comfortable, it works for them and for many this will be how life is with little if any issue.

But what about the other side....?

How many of our horses, if offered the (privilege?) of freedom, would choose to live in a stable/cave and close the door?

For the innate horse, the horse that knows his inner ways and understands the need for his own freedom - how many of our horse's would choose this in their lives? Likely not many...

In the wild a horse will choose to seek his own shelter, he may roam many miles in order to find a forest that offers him the leafy branches over head in order to lessen the harsh rainfall. He may roam and find himself a windbreak in some other natural form should he feel the need for shelter.

He may choose to seek out, or even stumble across a fixed natural form that closes him in, but will enable him an exit in which to run through in order to escape - should he feel the need. In reality he will never fully close himself in - why would he? His vulnerability and self preservation knows better.

To shut himself in would cause him physical and in many cases mental vulnerability. Should a fire break out - how would he flee? - He knows better than to put himself at this kind of risk.

OK so you visit your horse everyday at 7pm, you turn him out and come back again at 7pm and put him back in his stable the same as you have done for years. But how does he know that just because you came back and let him out those times, that you will this time? - He doesn't. He just has to trust (if he can) that you will.

As always there is another side to this which is the horse that seeks comfort in his stable. The horse that *knows* you will be back. Knows he will not have to stand out cold and shivering in the elements and that knows his dinner is soon coming as is some quality time before you go. In the full knowledge that in the morning you will return and further his trust in the routine of comfort that you have created for him. His stable means that he knows that he will not be bullied off his hay and that he can lie down safely without another herd member bothering him. This horse finds comfort in the stable that offers to him these things he may feel he needs.

Then we have the institutionalised horse. The one so used to his routine of out of stable to work, back to stable for the next twenty three hours until such a time as he is expected to work again before being locked in until the next time. Some of these horses have learnt - through no fault of their own - that safety may only be felt in their stable, safety both physically and mentally. These horses may dread and even fear the owner that comes to remove them from their comfort, the work and pain that they know comes next and may only be too happy for the bolt on the door to slide shut once again. For some of these horses the outside world of which they have seen little of can be scary. Such is the psychology that has now become theirs - through no fault of their own.

Several years ago, due to major illness, I had to box rest one of my ponies for a prolonged time. Smithy was a bit of an odd little pony that never quite fitted in with the rest of the herd. He was often 'told off' by the others for his incessant annoying behaviour and pestering. Before this time he had never been shut in a stable before, but due his illness and discomfort and his focus on that, little notice was paid by him to the fact he was closed in. Sadly it was eight long weeks of recovery before Smithy was able to be turned back out. This was when I made an interesting observation. Each evening when I went out to feed my horses, Smithy would follow me to the yard and wait quietly by the stable door and ask to be let in and he would spend the night in his stable. From here on in, this became the routine of his own choosing, one that continued until the end of his days. There was no forced incarceration, he had simply decided and felt that his stable provided him over night, what being with his herd didn't.

Whether we choose to stable our horse's or not is so often beyond our control and all too often when we do have a choice it becomes beyond their control - they simply must go along with our decision.

Stables may bring comfort, rest, reassurance as much as they can bring fear, turmoil and the closing down and retreat of the fragile equine psyche.

Due to this there is no hard and fast rule when it comes to stabling and the emotional feelings of horses that can be applied to *all*. Each situation and each individual horse needs to be given unique and careful consideration.

As humans with financial constraints we may have little say over if we choose to live in a mansion, a large or small house, a flat, caravan or even a cardboard box. In many cases due to this our horse's and what will are able to provide for them due to our finances, or what is available option wise to us, is often beyond both ours and their control. Yet let us not forget that that which is available to us is not always what we would choose for ourselves. How many have chosen to leave their mansion with little other than the clothes on their back and move into a caravan or even a cardboard box? Whilst such actions may seem strange to many of us, it is within that individual's own mind to know what they need, what suits them and where they are best happy. This is the same with horses. Just because a plush stable with a deep bed is available to our horse, this does not mean that he would not instead choose a muddy field with his friends and other herd members if he is offered the chance.

My own horses are kept in such a way that they have freedom to move. No matter which field they are in, they are able to walk to their yard where they have a large field shelter and open double stable with no partition. Here they will find their slow hay feeders and they are able to put themselves in and out as they so wish. Ideally from an early age this is the life that will benefit most horses. It aids in their social life and enables them to make decisions over the weather and companionship for themselves. It enables them to live as near to nature as is able to safely be provided for them and it aids their health - both mental and physical. But should our horse fall ill, or badly injure himself in such a way that box rest is needed. It is also of utmost importance that he is able to feel comfortable in a stable in order that stress and anxiety does not hold him back in his recovery.

So sad are the videos posted on social media sites of horses that are weaving and box walking and laughed at, as the ignorant laugh and say they are dancing. Have these people no conscious and compassion towards the mental torture that these horses are going through that is likely to be their everyday life from which there is no escape.

How many people choose not to stable their horses solely because their hind legs fill due to lack of movement? Failing to recognise the medical issue their horse has that in many cases will be down to a lack of electrolytes or an imbalance of them?

Personally for me, stabling vs living out is about the individual's freedom. The freedom of choice, not just over movement - but also of mind. It is for this reason that my horse's will always be able to make their choice, for now their choice is freedom in the form of living out and freedom to choose when to come in.

Would I choose to lock in a stable a horse? No, I would enable and listen to my horse's choice over if he felt this were best for him.

There will always be limitations both financial and in our options available as to how we are able to keep our horse's. But within that, we also have the freedom to make choice and create change. It may just be that your horse would like to leave his plush stable and live with the scruffy unrugged horses out in the elements down the road. The ones that huddle around the field shelter keeping each other warm in the cold wet weather. By the same token, those horses may wish to leave, be groomed everyday and enjoy the routine of the plush stable life.

Each horse is his own being with his own emotional and physical needs.

Who are we to take that choice from him and force our own will on him?

Let us make the best decisions *on behalf* of our horse that we are able, let us make life as comfortable as we can for him and leave his options open to change as he changes. He offers us so much in return yet he asks for little from us.

Let us do the best we can for him in all ways.

THE HORSE'S ENERGY AWARENESS

Many of us have heard the term 'energy awareness' and yet do not have a full understanding of what this means. When this is the case, it is likely due to us not being particularly energy aware ourselves. We are all individuals and we will all have varying and different sensitivity levels in regards to what is going on around us and is in the atmosphere - it is the same with horses.

Some horses will without a doubt be more sensitive to others and that, dependent on their environment and living conditions, will play a role in how they feel. There is no hard and fast rule for how a sensitive and energy aware horse will present outwardly. It is not just the level of their sensitivity that plays a part in their outward demeanour, but also their personality as well.

Since the beginning of my work and introduction to horses, it has become very apparent as to just how perceptive they can be. It is not unheard of for a quiet horse to suddenly become upset out hacking, as they are asked to go past a disused slaughter barn, or for them to react when coming into contact with other naturally energies such as ley lines.

Symptoms may include:

Anxiety, stopping or becoming upset and always at the same spot for no apparent reason

Stopping and lowering their head and worrying about walking forwards for no apparent reason

Spinning, backing up or rearing suddenly

Focusing on objects such as buildings that usually would not bother them and refusing to go past them, or hurrying past

They may experience:

Tingling sensations

Feelings of dread

A change in atmospheric pressure

Temperature changes

Stimulation of their nervous system

Irrational fear and anxiety

We only have to look back to the tsunami of ten years ago and how the animals that were able to, made their way to higher ground long before many humans were aware of the monstrous waves that were to hit and cause such devastation. As already mentioned, naturally occurring energies such as ley lines may have an affect on some horses, as will changes in air pressure, some electrical appliances and overhead cables. If we stand next to a radio with our mobile phone, we are able to hear the distorted signals caused and how it has an affect on the radio waves. Many horses are aware of mobile phones in the same way, as well as feeling the change before they ring. In some cases due to this some horses will react in someway *before* your phone even rings. When horses experience many of these things, they do not always understand them. Whilst some horses may not react it does not mean that these sensations are not being felt, only that it is of no concern to them.

However, it is not just 'things' that can cause the mood or level of concern to change for our horses. People along with the horse's herd companions will also have an affect on them.

Think for a moment back to when you last met or had a conversation with someone that was calm. They walked into the room and you instantly felt better. They may have had a soft voice that instantly helped you to relax and feel comfortable with them. Now let us think back to an opposite experience. The last time we spoke to someone that made you feel uncomfortable. They may not have said or done anything unkind to you, but just due to the harsh energy that they emitted was enough to make you feel uncomfortable in their presence.

Horses have little choice in where they live and who they live with. Their owners are chosen for them, their friends, where they live and how they live. When they feel uncomfortable with someone or something and are unable to be able to remove themselves from that environment, the anxiety that this may cause for them can snowball. They are stuck - they can not heal themselves – nor can they escape.

Imagine being brought up for sixteen years by a parent that beats you, even the sound of hearing a key in the door as a sign that they are home and about to come into contact with you could have been enough to start that anxiety to stir within you. Even if no physical harm occurred, a harsh voice and lack of compassion and kind touch can be enough to destroy those sixteen years. You may choose to leave the home as often as you can or even permanently. You may choose to seek the council of others, voice your upset and find comfort outside your situation from a kind hearted person - or even your horse.

Sadly horses to a large degree in relation to their lives are under our 'control'. For this reason and the laws of 'ownership' they may never be fortunate enough to be able to find relief in other relationships, or be able to remove themselves, even if only for an hour. From the harsh environment they find themselves in.

Is it any wonder so many horses suffer from anxiety?

Think for a moment, how are you around your horse?

Do you leave your emotional baggage at the gate before you go and see him?

Do you carry it through the gate and dump it at your horse's feet?

Do you stop to say 'hello' to him?

Do you acknowledge him - or too a large degree is he invisible to you other than when you are wanting something from him?

Should he suddenly get upset how do you react?

Do you slap him - pull at his lead rope?

Do you breathe out and seek to reassure him?

How you choose to react, how you feel and how you portray that in your demeanour, as well as what you hide, will all be felt by your horse. You may be able to put up living with you, but can he?

In simple terms he is stuck with you, he has no choice and how his life is, how he experiences and if his needs are met (both emotional and physical) or not, that is largely down to you – and so often beyond his control.

ABOUT THE AUTHOR

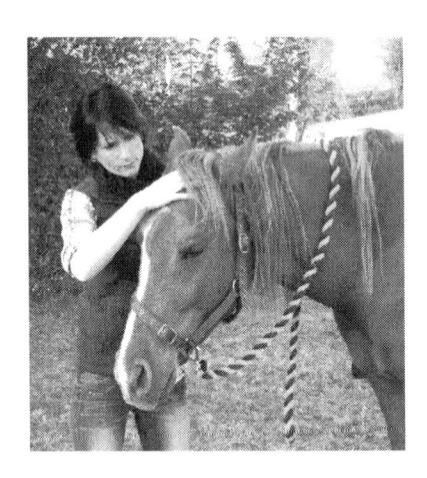

Holly has been working as a professional Animal Communicator and Therapist since 1999. She currently lives in Wales with her seven cats and three Arabian horses.

She is the Author of many books and courses on animal therapies and horsemanship. These are available throughout the UK as well as internationally.

She has a keen interest in natural behaviour and medicine as well as, psychological disorders in animals and Neuroscience. A huge amount of her time is spent helping people to understand their animals, aid in their recovery and create a better life for them.

Holly was one of the first Animal Communicators to teach workshops in England and is the Author of the first recognised Animal Communication Diploma in the UK.

Her accredited courses are available through Stonebridge College, links for which can be found on her website.

For information about Holly's other books, please visit:

www.hollydavis.co.uk

COMING IN 2015

Horsemanship - Creating the Magic

******

NOW AVAILABLE

Horsemanship – Myth Magic and Mayhem

More Horsemanship books to come in 2015

Keep a look out!

RESOURCES

Holly Davis
Animal Communicator and Therapist
Natural Medicine and Behaviour
Equine Specialist
Tel: 01994 241255
www.hollydavis.co.uk

Sue Gardner
Human & Horse Trainer
Author of Applied Equine Behaviour Home Study Courses
Helping Humans understand their Horses
Private & group training sessions
Workshops & Lectures
Author of Applied Equine Behaviour Home Study Courses
www.suegardner.co.uk
www.appliedequinebehaviour.co.uk
Email: suegardneruk@yahoo.co.uk
Tel: 01903 235743
Mobile: 07813 813386

Avis Senior
BHSAI – Reiki
Author of Horse Riding Choose Your Weapons
www.avissenior.com

Camille Dareau
Holistic riding, training and horse care
www.happy-horse-training.com

Elenore Bowden-Bird
Aulanda Park Liberty
www.apequineliberty.com.au

Graeme Green
Horse Healing and Land Healing
www.themindfulhorse.wordpress.com

Susan Duckworth
Hoofboots, Bitless Bridles, Neem and much more.
www.bitlessandbarefoot.com

Alan Howell
Medical Grade Essential Oils and Aromatics
www.shechina.co.uk

Thunderbrook
Organic and Natural Horse Feeds and Educational Articles
www.thunderbrook.co.uk
Terry Shubrook
Kinesiology and Healing
www.terryshubrook.co.uk

The Masterson Method
www.mastersonmethod.com

Victoria Standen
Zoopharmocognosy / Animal Aromatics
www.harmonyhealingforanimals.co.uk

Liz Harris
McTimoney, Massage, Reiki
www.lizharris.co.uk

Suzanna Thomas
Centre for workshops and holistic horse care and products
www.spiritofthenaturalhorse.com

Henry Cumming
Horse Healing and Whispering
www.henrycumming.com

Kirsty Cooper
Horse Hair Jewellery
www.finedesignequinegifts.co.uk

Teresa Perrin
Bowen Therapy
www.teresaperrin.co.uk

Kay Emmerson
Sports Massage, Equine Aromatics, Kinesiology
www.equine-therapeutics.co.uk

Dawn Cox
Horse Rhythm Beads
www.angelhorse.co.uk

Helen Jacks - Hewett
McTimoney, Sports Massage
www.horse-back.co.uk

Rosie Hume
Masterson Method
Norfolk and North Suffolk
Tel: 07786 545977
Email: rosie3319@gmail.com

Lou Wilks
Masterson Method
www.naturallyhorse.co.uk

Julie Dexter
EMRT Bowen and Crystal Healing
www.bowenbalancing.co.uk

Emma Knowles
Veterinary Physiotherapy and Equine Touch
emma4et@hotmail.com
07921258752

www.theequinetouch.com

www.navp.co.uk

Printed in Great Britain
by Amazon.co.uk, Ltd.,
Marston Gate.